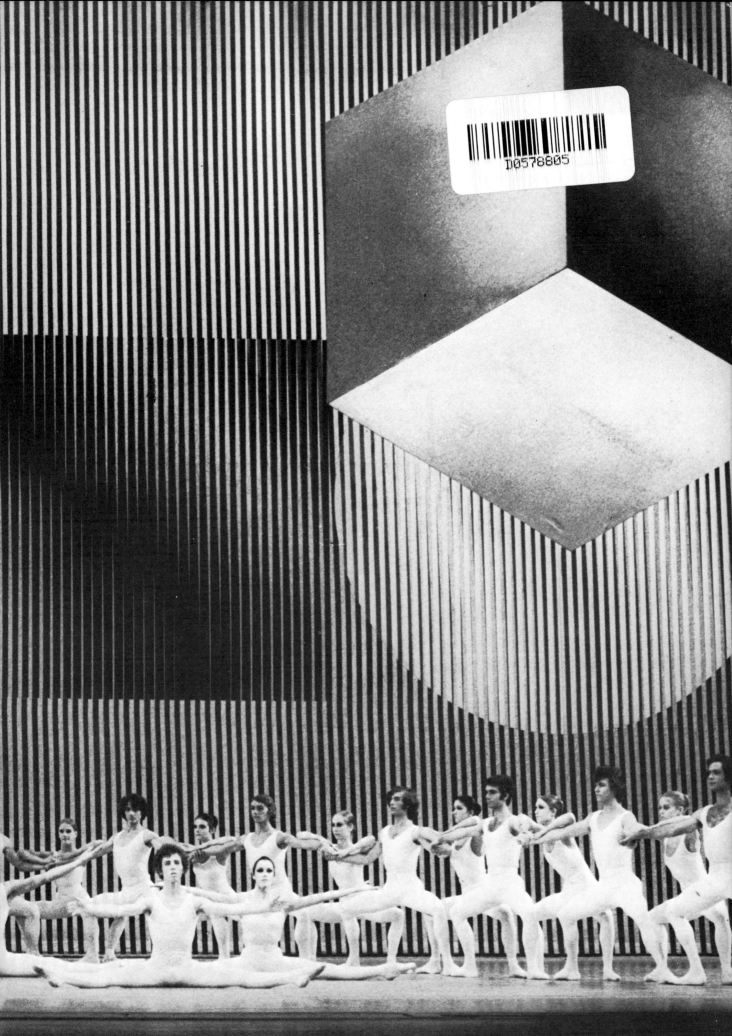

Ballet&
Modern
Dance

Ballet &

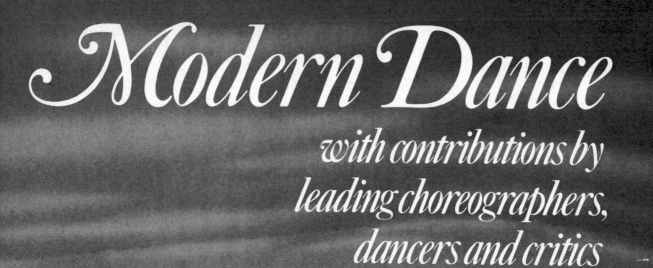

Modern Dance

with contributions by leading choreographers, dancers and critics

Octopus Books

Contents

Half-title: Montage of Peter Schaufuss and Maria Guerrero in Nutcracker

Right: Antoinette Sibley and Anthony Dowell in Jerome Robbins' Afternoon of a Faun

Title page: The Rite of Spring by Maurice Béjart

Lincoln Kirstein

The New York City Ballet

*T*HE NEW YORK CITY BALLET CAME INTO
being in 1948. It was the result of labors since
1934, on the part of George Balanchine and
Lincoln Kirstein towards the formation of a
permanent American company, dedicated to the pro-
mulgation of the traditional academic classic theatrical
dance. In 1948, under the leadership of Morton Baum, it
received the sponsorship of the New York City Center of
Music and Drama, Inc., a charitable, non-profit, tax-
exempt institution, of whom the Mayor of the City is,
ex officio, the President. It enjoys a modest subsidy by way
of rental from the municipality, and other aid from State
and Federal sources, private foundations and citizen
groups. The permanent home of the New York City Ballet
is the State Theater in Lincoln Center for the Performing
Arts, designed for it by Philip Johnson, which it shares
with the New York City Opera Company for half the year.
It regularly gives two annual seasons, Fall-Winter and
Spring-Summer, November-February and May-June. In
July it appears at the Performing Arts Center, Saratoga
Springs, New York, and in August in Wolftrap Farm,
near Washington, Ravinia, near Chicago and either Cleve-
land or Los Angeles in alternating years.

The company numbers around ninety dancers, most of
whom were prepared since childhood at the School of
American Ballet, a non-profit educational institution,
housed in, but independent from the Juilliard School at
Lincoln Center. The School was founded in 1934 and
presently has an annual registration of some five hundred
students, summer and winter. Through a generous
grant-in-aid from the Ford Foundation, it supports
local scholarships in affiliated schools across the United
States, and offers advanced instruction to gifted pupils
from these and other sources.

The School and Company have been governed by
George Balanchine and staffs chosen and/or trained by
him. Born in 1904, he entered the Imperial Ballet School
in Saint Petersburg in 1914, graduating from the Soviet
State Academy in 1921. After study at the Musical
Conservatory, he emigrated to the West, and joined
the Ballets Russes of Serge Diaghilev, whose last ballet-
master he became in 1924, serving him until his death in
1929. Subsequently he served the Royal Danish Ballet in
Copenhagen, and as ballet-master for the Theatre de
Monte Carlo in 1932. Invited by Lincoln Kirstein and
Edward Warburg, he came to New York in late 1933, to
found a school and a company. Successive organizations
from 1934 through 1941, for which the School of American Ballet largely provided dancers and Balanchine the
choreographic repertory were The American Ballet, the
American Ballet Caravan, and, as of 1947, Ballet Society, a
private organization to produce lyric theater.

Since its inception as The American Ballet, the company
has been distinguished by a close association with the
compositions and personal influence of Igor Stravinsky.
The ballets *Jeux des Cartes* (1937), *Orpheus* (1947),
Agon (1957), were commissioned by Balanchine and
Kirstein, and some dozen other ballets of Stravinsky's

scores are included in the extant repertory. A week-long
festival in June 1972, gave a conspectus, in depth of this
seminal composer's life-work. Balanchine's devotion to
Stravinsky has been important also to the dancers'
understanding of progressive music, the development of
their understanding of new ways of moving and gesturing,
according to new principles of rhythm and metric.
Perhaps the most characteristic element in the progress of
the New York City Ballet is its attention to the musical
sub-structure. Balanchine believes that music is essentially
the floor of the dance, and that without musical suggestion
the result is largely an inconsiderable improvisation. Hence
the repertory of the company has been eclectic, om-
niverous and surprising, embracing a wide choice of
unfamiliar past works and popular (and unpopular, or
unfamiliar) contemporary scores.

With few exceptions, the New York City Ballet has no
dependance on the acknowledged 19th-century repertory,
dominantly the three principal "classic full-length"
ballets, *Giselle*, *Swan Lake* (except for a recension of
Act II), or *The Sleeping Beauty*. However, for many years,
it has presented an elaborate version of Tchaikovsky's
Nutcracker, in a new version by Balanchine and Jerome
Robbins, as well as a full-length *Midsummer Night's Dream*
with various music by Mendelssohn, and a full-length
Don Quixote with music by Nicholas Nabokov.

The choreographic philosophy of the company has been
dictated by Balanchine and Jerome Robbins, although
other choreographers have been notably associated with
the repertory. Among these have been and are, Sir

Previous pages: left: Jean-Pierre
Bonnefous and Karen von
Aroldingen in Balanchine's Violin
Concerto—*one of the works per-*
formed as part of the New York

City Ballet's Stravinsky Festival
week in 1972. Right: John Clifford
and Linda Yourth in Balanchine's
production of Stravinsky's
Danses Concertantes

Frederick Ashton, Todd Bolender, John Butler, John Clifford, Merce Cunningham, Lorca Massine, Francisco Moncion, Richard Tanner and the Christensen brothers, Lew and William. John Taras, a well-known ballet-master all over Europe and the United States, has long been associated with the company as dancer and choreographer. In 1950, Jerome Robbins joined the company as solo dancer and choreographer. He returned as a principal collaborator after many years on his own with a personal company and working in films and on Broadway. He has recently enriched the repertory by capital additions, notably *Dances at a Gathering*, *Goldberg Variations*, *Watermill*, as well as revivals of his *Concert* and *Afternoon of a Faun*.

The emphasis of the repertory of the New York City Ballet has been on the progression of the tradition of virtuosity in the academic idiom as born in North Italy in the late Renaissance, which was developed by contact and influence successively from France, Austria, Russia and England. When Balachine came to the United States he brought with him representative veterans of the Russian Imperial and State schools—notably Pierre Vladimiroff, Anatol Oboukhoff, Felia Doubrovska, and later Alexandra Danilova. These were joined by Muriel Stuart, an English dancer trained by Anna Pavlova, and more recently by Stanley Williams, the well-known dancer and teacher from the Royal Danish Ballet. Soviet-trained dancers, as well as ex-dancers of the New York City Ballet Company, form a strong teaching staff, and this is responsible for the style, discipline and technique that is seen on stage.

Above left: George Balanchine

Above: Allegra Kent and Jacques d'Amboise in Balanchine's Scotch Symphony

Top right: Patricia McBride in A Midsummer Night's Dream *by Balanchine*

Right: Diana Adams and Arthur Mitchell in Balanchine's Agon

9

Above: Members of the New York City Ballet in Jerome Robbins' *ballet to Bach's* Goldberg Variations

Top right: Allegra Kent and Anthony Blum in Jerome Robbins' *ballet to Stravinsky's* Dumbarton Oaks *concerto*

Right: Kay Mazzo in Balanchine's Violin Concerto

10

Above: Melissa Hayden, Jean-Pierre Bonnefous and Francisco Moncion in Balanchine's Orpheus

Left: Gelsey Kirkland and Sara Leland in Balanchine's Concerto Barocco

Right: Patricia Neary and Anthony Blum in Balanchine's Four Temperaments

Next pages: top: Mimi Paul and Bruce Marks in the duet from Massine's Gaieté Parisienne
Below: Carla Fracci and Erik Bruhn in the duet from Bournonville's Flower Festival at Genzano

The presentations of the company depend so greatly on music that it has been fortunate in the services of a musical director of the distinction of Robert Irving, formerly with the Royal Ballet, but who has been with the New York dancers since 1953. He has developed a symphonic ensemble of considerable authority and prestige. The scores used by Stravinsky, Schoenberg, Charles Ives, Mayezumi, Xenakis, as well as the more familiar works of Bach, Bizet, Brahms, Gounod and Tchaikovsky, require considerable preparation. A notable addition to the musical staff, particularly in the solo-piano ballets of Jerome Robbins, are the skills and brilliance of Gordon Boelzner. A very considerable number of scores have been commissioned directly from their composers, and a number exist which have, as yet, not been produced. Notable among these is *The Birds of America*, a full-length ballet by the distinguished American composer, Morton Gould, based on the character of John James Audubon, the great bird-painter which is projected towards the Bicentennial celebrations of 1976. Iannis Xenakis has finished a second ballet for the company, and there are further additions to the already large Stravinsky repertory.

The profile of the New York City Ballet has largely been determined by the character, talent and philosophy of George Balanchine, together with a complementary contribution from Jerome Robbins in recent years. Balanchine's preference has been and remains towards an athleticism of mind and body, and impersonality in presentation. Just as he has limited the repertory to the invention of new works, so has he consistently refused to promulgate "stars"; he has believed that "personality", more often than not, while recognizable and hence saleable in advance, is a professional deformation, and that the star-dancer is often more interested in the projection of idiosyncratic mannerism than the pattern or perfection of dancing as such. While the negotiable prestige of stardom has been ignored, there has been a consequent emphasis on the ensemble of dancers, which was formerly known, and discounted as a *corps de ballet*. Balanchine has believed that the *corps* is indeed the body of ballet, and its membership enlist only dancers who might once have been termed "soloists". The promotion of the corps to the position of eminence is a chief characteristic of the repertory. In the 19th century, it was a simple background for the framing or relaxation of star ballerinas. In the 20th, due largely to Balantine's insistent innovations, the ensemble assumes an interest and importance equal to the action and appeal of soloists. The corps thus becomes what is, in essence, an aggregation of soloists, performing on a heightened level of activity and interest.

Similarly, the New York City Ballet, while on occasion enjoying the benefits of the rich imagination of painters like Eugene Berman, Esteban Frances and Pavel Tcheitchev, as well as the sculptor Isamu Noguchi and the scenic

designer Rouben Ter-Arutunian, has not been notable for its accentuation of the decorative or cosmetic attributes of stage-production. A deliberately sparse or Spartan manner of presentation has been adopted in general, as much from choice as from economic necessity. Focus, aim and accent has been on the projection of the three-dimensional plasticity of the human body, based on interesting disposition and measurement from a musically patterned basis. In the half-century of his working life, Balanchine has amplified the language of movement and gesture, past any previous limits, increasing the uses of the idiom while cleaving to the long descent of traditional academic training.

The New York City Ballet has performed in the principal cities of the United States on a variety of occasions,

Previous page: right: Natalia Makarova as Swanilda in Ballet Theater's Coppélia

Top: Edward Villella as the central figure in Jerome Robbins' Watermill

although its touring is restricted by the increasing cost of transportation, and the lack of audiences capable of supporting a practical season of performances. However, generally with aid from the United States Department of State, the company has appeared with success twice in the Soviet Union, and in Japan, Israel, Australia, England, Scotland and the main European countries, including Poland and Greece. Balanchine's own repertory has been given to most of the regional companies of the United States and Canada, while it is also seen constantly in the opera-houses of Britain and Europe. The New York City Ballet Company has achieved a measure of stability and permanence, possibly as great as can be imagined for an institution lacking absolute government subsidy and accreditation.

Right : Chopiniana *is a staging of the Fokine ballet known in Europe as* Les Sylphides. *The New York City Ballet dance it in practice dress: Kay Mazzo (left) in the Prelude*

Left: The Concert is a romp by Jerome Robbins in which the audience at a Chopin recital live out their private fantasies

Below: The Cage by Jerome Robbins depicts a colony of ferocious and dominating female insects

Bottom: Jerome Robbins' Requiem Canticles was the final ballet danced at the New York City Ballet's Stravinsky Festival in June 1972

Marcia B. Siegel

American Dance

AMERICAN DANCE HAS ALWAYS DEFINED itself by its creators more than by its producing institutions. The strength and vitality of our dance, its ability to appeal to many audiences, depend, I think, on the relative unimportance of tradition and the machineries of tradition here. Relatively few companies exist to serve tradition compared to those that express one artist's vision.

The New York City Ballet, probably our foremost dance organization, is the province of George Balanchine and only incidentally the New York stronghold of classical ballet. Its repertory is substantially a Balanchine repertory amplified by a few other choreographers, its dancers are trained to do Balanchine's neo-classic style, and the entire public stance of the company reflects Balanchine's artistic convictions. Ballet Theater, alone of our principal companies, was founded to continue a tradition—that of the old Russian repertory companies—rather than to perform someone's choreography.

Institutions have not proved hospitable places to adventurous young dancers, from the time when Martha Graham, Doris Humphrey and Charles Weidman left Denishawn in the late 1920s. Perhaps an institution's commitment to preserving an established style doesn't allow it to harbor serious contradictions of that style. At least in this country, almost every choreographic innovator has had to go through a more or less torturous break with his teachers or his home company, and has had to develop a new company as his own instrument.

Now, with half a century of free-wheeling, chaotic, highly creative achievement behind us, American dance seems to be moving toward formalization and codification of its earlier discoveries. Dance is looking for bigger audiences, and as the audiences increase, so does the accessibility and predictability of the dance form. Government funding of dance has become essential to survival, and in the intense competition for the always insufficient funds, companies are under increasing pressure to demonstrate their business responsibility, to give at least an appearance of permanence. Although box office receipts cannot be counted on to cover financial deficits, the box office does reflect the size of the audience, and audience numbers have become a crucial bargaining token in the competition for subsidies.

At the same time, the age of individualism is on the wane, as the pioneers of modern dance and modern ballet leave the scene. Instead of remaining on the stage, where they personify the styles they have developed, many choreographers are retiring quite young from dancing, and many are no longer insisting on doing all the choreography for their companies. Diversity of repertory is coming into favor, rather than concentration on a single style. The parent-figure/hero/creator is out. The cooperative is in.

Still, it comes as a shock to hear dance students at a large university worrying about how they can make sure no one in their audiences will be bored. Even in the closed, non-commercial setting of a college campus, the need to find and please an audience is influencing dance. The powerful presences and distinctive styles of the early days are fading, but so is the possibility of surviving with only a limited audience, as even the greatest of them did.

* * * * *

People go to see dance for a variety of reasons, and most dance companies or producers aim to attract one or more of these potential audiences. None of these categories, of course, excludes the others, and no single dance event ever has only one kind of audience.

The subscription audience is committed to dance mainly as a necessary part of its cultural diet. The ballet subscriber—so far modern dance has not attracted this audience—also attends the opera, the theater, symphony concerts, museums. For the subscriber, I think, going to the ballet is the event. He considers the theater and its location as important as the company performing. He isn't too choosy about what he sees as long as it provides all the conventional satisfactions: attractive scenery and costumes, pleasant music, graceful dancing.

In New York, the subscriber accounts for a rather small proportion of the total dance audience, though some of the bigger companies rely heavily on his continuing patronage. But outside of New York, in cities and university towns

Previous page right: Gary Chryst in Arpino's Clowns performed by the Joffrey Ballet

Above: Pillar of Fire was one of the several important works that Antony Tudor staged for American Ballet Theater during its first seasons. Sallie Wilson is seen here as the central figure, Hagar, with Gayle Young
Right: Cynthia Gregory and Ted Kivitt in Antony Tudor's Dark Elegies

where less dance takes place, subscribers are more important. They usually represent the community's social and cultural leaders, and they look to the conservative subscriber-supported New York institutions as models for local efforts.

In New York it appears that the largest segment of the dance audience is looking for entertainment. This audience might go to the theater or the auto show or the circus as readily as it goes to dance. Unlike the subscription audience, these patrons are unpredictable. They don't plan their visits in advance, and they probably follow reviews, advertisements, and other publicity quite carefully.

This is the audience that adores pop dance—any dance form, ballet, modern or in between, that is technically exciting and topically recognizable. Since it doesn't make a season-long commitment to any one company, this audience doesn't demand much of the repertory, it cares more for stylishness than style, and it reveres few of the values that dance companies are organized to uphold: continuity, creative achievement, aesthetic form.

Another large group of patrons, both in New York and outside of it, is the balletomanes, dancers and dance students, and partisans of certain dancers or companies who used to be thought of as "the dance audience". This group does care for the continuity and creativity of dance as an art, but it may be extremely selective in the way it defines these terms. "The dance audience" can always be counted on for its presence, and perhaps for this reason, its tastes are not catered to. Once a year or so, Ballet Theater will put together an all-Tudor program for "the dance audience" but the rest of the time it finds its own favorites.

The government's growing investment in dance has carried with it a mandate to engage the interest of various ethnic and non-middle-class groups as audience. Reduced ticket prices, special buses from ghetto neighborhoods and schools, educational programs and performances have been aimed at bringing these new audiences into the theater. Predictably, the black and ethnic dance companies have had great success with this audience, not only because of racial identification, but because they are offering a political message specifically directed to the black and minority group viewer.

More and more black dance—that is, theater dance that is being done primarily by and for blacks—is trying to reach out to its own community with representational, theatrical forms that make very obvious connections to the rising black consciousness. Although most black companies would not refuse recognition by the white culture, they are turning away from integration as a goal.

The last large, definable portion of the dance audience is the art devotees. This group will attend any dance that might be an important artistic event, or will look for artistic merit above all in a dance performance. This is, once again, a group fragmented by its tastes; it includes those

Top left: Fancy Free was Jerome Robbins' first ballet. It was created for American Ballet Theater in 1944, and the success of this brilliant study of three sailors on leave marked the arrival of a major new choreographic talent.

Left: Christine Sarry as the cowgirl in Agnes de Mille's Rodeo

who dress up and give dinner parties for the opening of *Parade*, those who regularly support Merce Cunningham and Martha Graham, and those who sit on the loft and gallery floors to see far-out, experimental works by obscure choreographers.

In a heavy week, as many as 50 dance performances can be seen in New York, and there are seldom fewer than ten events to choose from. The audience can afford to be selective, and the range of attractions is tremendous.

*   *   *   *   *

If one dance company in the United States can be said to be secure, it is the New York City Ballet, although even that security is predicated on the continuing presence of heavy subsidies and George Balanchine. The company performs five to six months of the year in its own New York State Theater at Lincoln Center, and does shorter seasons during the summer at Saratoga Springs, N.Y., and other festivals. Although it seldom publishes a company roster, NYCB carries about 80 dancers, most of them drawn from its School of American Ballet, which is located in the new Juilliard building at Lincoln Center.

The Balanchine repertory is a stupendous achievement, for its longevity and its range, its profundity of expression and its endlessly resourceful use of the classical vocabulary. Balanchine has had a succession of female protégées, and at present he has brought Patricia McBride, Allegra Kent and Kay Mazzo to the peak of their careers. Newest of the Balanchine baby ballerinas is Gelsey Kirkland, who promises to follow superlatively in the tradition.

The Balanchine dancer, in addition to being a technical wonder, is musical, understated (some call her inexpressive), intelligent in a dance sense. She projects a special feeling of self-sufficiency; it's as if, having created her, Balanchine gave her the extra gift of independence. She doesn't beg for the audience's favor or show off, she just does the dance and it becomes her dance.

Now nearly 70, Balanchine might be expected to slacken off and supply just enough novelty to keep the subscribers loyal. Instead, he produced several fine works in the past year, and he seems to have developed a new interest in choreographing for men. A not inconsiderable element in the success of NYCB's extraordinary Stravinsky Festival in June 1972 was the dancing of Helgi Tomasson in Divertimento from *Baiser de la Fée* and Peter Martins in *Duo Concertant*, and of Edward Villella in *Pulcinella* (co-choreographed by Balanchine and Jerome Robbins). Balanchine capitalized on the virtuosity of Tomasson, the romanticism of Martins, and Villella's growing gift for character, much as he has often choreographed for the special qualities of his women.

Despite the continuing vitality of Balanchine, the future of NYCB depends on who will succeed him as artistic director. Jerome Robbins has choreographed

Top right: Schubertiade *by Michael Smuin*
Centre: José Limón's The Moor's Pavane *is an interpretation of* Othello: *Bruce Marks as Othello,* *Royes Fernandez as Iago, Cynthia Gregory as Desdemona and Sallie Wilson as Emilia*
Right: American Ballet Theater in Alvin Ailey's The River

four major works for the company since 1967, in addition to his contributions to the Stravinsky Festival, and is thought to be a prime candidate.

Of all the creative giants of American dance, only Jerome Robbins has made a successful career without one particular company to choreograph on; his parallel work in the commercial theater has afforded him financial independence as well as a supplementary outlet for his talents. He could work in the concert field more or less on inspiration, and he has often been known to sketch and revise a new ballet for years before finally setting it. Perhaps this method of working explains why Robbins doesn't have a clear choreographic style. He hasn't had to repeat or refine the approaches that worked in order to please an audience or identify himself to his audience, so he could freely explore the possibilities of jazz, folk, romantic, classical, and even avant-garde ideas in his ballets.

Robbins' work has always been very successful with NYCB audiences, even the slow, attenuated, quasi-Oriental *Watermill*, which is so much more a visual than a dance experience. His eye for theater has enriched the NYCB repertory, but the company would probably lose its present focus quickly under his less concentrated leadership.

It would be ironic, though not entirely illogical, to see

Top: David Blair of the Royal Ballet staged Swan Lake *for Ballet Theater: Eleanora d'Antuono and Ted Kivitt are seen in the last act*

Left: Cynthia Gregory and Michael Denard (a guest from the Paris Opéra) in Ballet Theater's version of the Grand Pas *from Minkus's* Paquita

Robbins end up in the academic, single-minded New York City Ballet rather than the less stable, more catholic American Ballet Theater where he started. Featuring no single choreographer, Ballet Theater was founded in 1940 to present a diversified repertory, and it continues this policy, with the great Russian classics, 20th-century European works, and Americana forming the backbone of its repertory.

Without a home theater or an annual performance season staked out in New York, Ballet Theater often shows the strain of its constant touring, audience-building, money-raising efforts. The company includes some fine young dancers, who are sometimes permitted to play for sensationalism rather than subtlety. What is emphasized among ABT's accomplishments over the years can swing wildly, from a spate of big classics—*Swan Lake, Giselle, Coppelia*—to Diaghilev revivals—*Petrushka, Le Spectre de la Rose*; from big imported superstars Erik Bruhn, Carla Fracci, Natalia Makarova and Paolo Bortoluzzi to glamorous, home-grown Cynthia Gregory. Ballet Theater can present probably more ballets by more choreographers than any other company, though it sometimes does them badly.

It's easy to get the impression, as ballet lovers often do, that Ballet Theater is making one last desperate effort to stay alive, and if that fails, the company must simply disintegrate. But there always seems to be a new approach; Ballet Theater thrives on new approaches, in fact. The company seems most valuable to me when it is incubating a new choreographer, as it did with Eliot Feld in 1967–68. Feld, like Robbins 20 years before him, made his first, hugely successful ballets for ABT, and then left for greener pastures. After the collapse of his two-year-old American Ballet Company, Feld returned to ABT for a season and is now free-lancing.

Feld showed so much daring with his Ballet Theater works *Harbinger* and *At Midnight*, and with the first dances he did for his own company, that his present retreat into rigid formality and stark showmanship seems almost the act of another person. Feld's two Stravinsky works for Ballet Theater in 1972, *A Soldier's Tale* and *Eccentrique*, and his 1973 *Jive* for the Joffrey Ballet were as dogmatic and regimented as his early ballets had been liberating. Feld hasn't danced on the American stage since Ballet Theater's 1972 summer season, but some of his protégés, notably Christine Sarry and Daniel Levins, are achieving new scope and recognition with Ballet Theater.

One of the stringent pressures that eventually overwhelmed Feld's little company was the demand for repertory. Perhaps no one but a Balanchine can so thoroughly dominate a repertory and still keep his audience alive in these times. The American dance public and most of dance's critics are in no mood to examine one artist's work carefully and repeatedly.

Even the Robert Joffrey Ballet has begun revising its image as a one-choreographer company—although its resident choreographer, Gerald Arpino, is facile enough to provide unlimited styled-to-order ballets all by himself. Arpino, who is a co-founder of the company and assistant director, is a prototypal eclectic. With John Butler and Glen Tetley, whose backgrounds are primarily in modern dance, Arpino heads the large group of contemporary choreographers who borrow or adapt whatever movement style suits their purpose, rather than permitting a movement style to grow out of their own expressive needs.

In recent seasons Arpino has gunned his instinctive neo-Balanchinian classicism to orgiastic heights of speed and virtuosity. Such works as *Kettentanz* and *Chabriesque* demonstrate a kind of ultimate exploitation of the dancer's craft. Arpino's other ballets recently have used a variety of pop motifs: rock music (*Trinity*), prize fights (*Valentine*), gambling (*Jackpot*), and hippie love (*Sacred Grove on Mt. Tamalpais*).

The invariable triviality of Arpino's work has had a cloying effect on even the Joffrey audience, and Robert Joffrey has drawn increasingly on outside talent to improve his repertory. Since 1969 he has mounted *Three-Cornered Hat, Petrushka, Le Beau Danube* and *Parade*; has acquired ballets by Balanchine, Robbins and Feld; and has commissioned works from young choreographers. The Joffrey's extraordinary success in the spring 1973 season with *Deuce Coupe*, a truly innovative as well as a popular work, by the modern dancer Twyla Tharp, may lead to a change in the company's artistic fortunes.

*   *   *   *   *

Alvin Ailey was probably the first "purely" modern dancer to choreograph for a "pure" ballet company (*Feast of Ashes*, 1962, for the Joffrey when it was under the aegis of Rebekah Harkness). He also may be the first to choreograph a leading role for a classical ballerina and a modern dance company (*Flowers*, for his own company and Lynn Seymour, in 1971). In many ways Alvin Ailey personifies the blurring of distinctions between the two great dance ideologies, and the displacement of the individual artist-stylist by companies equipped to fulfill multiple audience needs.

Ailey made his name first as a chronicler of the black experience. With his funky little group, he carried an exuberant, sexy message out of the gospel churches and uptown streets to delighted audiences all over the world. About the mid-1960s, the company began increasing in size and technical prowess, and Ailey began adding the works of other choreographers to his repertory. His own movement style is a theatrically effective blend of Martha Graham twists and tensions, balletic elongations of line, and Afro-American energies. Now comprising nearly 25

superb dancers—ballet-trained, most of them—the Ailey company is our foremost non-classical repertory troupe.

Ailey no longer choreographs exclusively black or even modern dance works—he has done plotless ballets and semi-dramatic ballets for his own and other companies—but his earliest work fathered a whole "school" of black dance aimed at dramatizing certain aspects of black character and black history. Although he maintains an integrated company and a repertory that reaches into all areas of American dance, the Ailey performing style embodies a high-energy, extroverted self-confidence—part show business, part proselytizing, always exciting—that other black companies quickly adopted.

In 1972 Ailey's internationally acclaimed company joined the New York City and the Joffrey Ballets as a resident company of City Center. Ailey has made it. In his tremendous popularity, the superstar reputation of dancer Judith Jamieson, the mass media exposure the company constantly gets, young choreographers, black and white, see their dreams of pop success realized.

Increasing numbers of medium-sized companies are now distinguished by their performing rather than by their choreographic styles. This is partly due to economics: in order to receive what funding is available, a young choreographer has few alternatives to maintaining a strong permanent company that can tour a substantial part of the year. Eliot Feld's American Ballet Company's

fees were prohibitive because he refused to tour without an orchestra. He got few engagements and his dancers languished in New York between seasons. Ultimately he couldn't keep them together.

A company that spends much of its time on tour cannot build its audience gradually; it has to make contact at once, and often. Alvin Ailey learned this during his many foreign tours of the 1960s, as other modern dance companies are learning today. In recent years there has developed a sort of international style based on the expertise of today's young dancer. This style uses modern dance and ballet techniques, with intensified attack, focus, and timing, and a highly tuned sense of the ensemble. Decors, lighting, sound and costumes are imaginative and often quite splendid, while the choreography itself may be of minimal significance. Lar Lubovitch, Louis Falco and Paul Sanasardo head three of the most impressive companies employing this style.

In the spring of 1973, the number of professional dance companies eligible to receive federal government support for touring included 17 ballet companies in addition to the three I have discussed, ten large and about 50 smaller modern dance companies. Obviously, all of these are not run by Martha Graham. To shift the creative burden from a single artist, some companies have also spread out the choreographic responsibility. Ailey started doing this ten years ago; now Falco, Sanasardo and Bella Lewitsky

Above: Dancers of the Joffrey Ballet in Jerome Robbins' Interplay

Right: Revelations by Alvin Ailey with William Louther. This ballet is an expression of a simple faith that can be both joyful and penitent. (See over)

Revelations: *above, the company; left, Dudley Williams and right, Alvin Ailey with two members of his company*

are among the directors who have tried to diversify their repertories in accepting works by company members. Repertory Dance Theater of Utah, created in 1965 by the Rockefeller Foundation, goes even further by having no artistic director at all. The company is cooperatively run by its members, who share the work of teaching, choreographing, and rehearsing the works of outsiders.

* * * * *

A diminishing number of true modern dance innovators are still running their companies in the familiar pattern. In various ways, they all have met the problem of expanding their audiences. Alwin Nikolais' experimental years came just before the dance boom struck, and he was exceedingly fortunate to have Henry Street Playhouse to work in then. Tucked away on the Lower East Side of New York, the Playhouse accommodated less than 300 people, so Nikolais could play to several weekends of full houses without great expense or undue visibility. About 1968 he began making a transition to larger theaters, and by 1970 he moved his entire teaching and rehearsing operation uptown to the Space, a converted church in the garment district. Nikolais' New York seasons are now given at City Center

or the handsome Brooklyn Academy opera house.

Perhaps because he no longer has such a perfectly integrated creating/performing situation, Nikolais hasn't produced any technological gems to equal *Somniloquy* (1967) or *Tent* (1968). His recent works place more emphasis on the dancer—but Nikolais' choreographic style isn't especially notable—and his splendid lighting, color, costume and projection ideas look more like subsidiary effects than elements in a whole organism. Nikolais is still a great theater man, though, and—as seems to be happening all over the dance field—his work attracts audiences because it is so much more interesting than most conventional theater.

Paul Taylor has also moved towards theatricality, and away from the good-natured but often mystifying pursuits of his earlier work. There is still a bizarre quality about even the most uncomplicated Taylor dances, and usually the peculiarity is sexual. *So Long Eden* has a hillbilly Adam, Eve and a character named Jake, dancing and pairing off in various combinations. *Big Bertha* is a graphic description of the depravity lurking behind the gentle smiles of an All-American family: Paul Taylor, Bettie de Jong and Carolyn Adams have given remarkable performances in this work. In *Agathe's Tale*, the demure

31

heroine gets involved in an orgy with Satan, Pan, and the Unicorn who is supposed to be protecting her virtue.

Taylor still makes a pure-dance piece occasionally in addition to these satires of plot and character, but his choreography is so clever, his jokes so explicit, and his dancers so calculating that his work is beginning to look very decadent indeed. Taylor is one of the last moderns left to have created a movement style that is uniquely his own, and all his dancers except the buoyant Carolyn Adams seem to be straining to preserve its fidelity.

Erick Hawkins has acquired an increasingly large and vociferous audience, particularly on the college campuses. I cannot account for Hawkins' success in dance terms, although many young dancers are among his ardent supporters—perhaps because his movement demands a lot of control but doesn't require the dancer to project outside himself. Dancers like to do it. To me his work is extremely bland. He treats space two-dimensionally, as a field to design on. His dynamics are minimal. His Oriental imagery is simplistic to the point of coyness. His dancers are effusively spiritual.

Every Hawkins concert is accompanied by a barrage of words—articles, interviews, program notes, beautifully produced booklets—from his co-workers and from out-siders—telling about what a profound experience Hawkins

The Alwin Nikolais company in Tent, *a theater-piece in which the tent of the title becomes a universe in which dancers live out their existence*

Right: Murray Louis *in* Tensile Involvement, *performed by the Alwin Nikolais company*

32

*Over top: Carla Fracci as Giselle
and Erik Bruhn as Albrecht in Act
I of David Blair's staging of
Giselle for American Ballet
Theater*

*Below: Jerome Robbins' version of
Stravinsky's Les Noces for
American Ballet Theater*

*Over: far right: Russell Saltzbach
as the boy in Arpino's Sacred
Grove on Mount Tamalpais
with the Joffrey Company*

dance is. Hawkins propaganda goes to people's heads, persuades them, cultifies them. I think it soothes the intellectual's suppressed consciousness and guilty neglect of his body.

* * * *

The real giants—the creators of modern dance—are declining or are already gone. José Limón died at the end of 1972 after a period of illness and relative inactivity. Limón did choreograph to the end, and in his last years produced a fine tribute to Isadora Duncan and one major work, *The Unsung,* a series of solos for men that memorializes the American Indian. Limón's company continued in existence after his death, touring Russia and Europe with his choreography. By that time, many of the best known Limón dancers had left to form their own companies, and some of those who remained were concertizing independently during slow periods. Without their leader, these young dancers may find it hard to sustain their allegiance to his repertory.

Perhaps the best hope for the preservation of Limón's work is its incorporation into the repertory of other companies. *The Moor's Pavane,* his undisputed masterpiece, has already been adopted by Ballet Theater and a number of other companies. Limón's best work presents such a clear choreographic design and at the same time such a dramatic challenge to the dancers that it seems to have quite a good chance of survival. With Doris Humphrey, Charles Weidman, Martha Graham, Anna Sokolow, and others whose styles were more personal, more unusual, the problem is going to be more difficult.

Many of Doris Humphrey's dances have been notated, but less than a generation after her death, the rhythmic impulse that underlay her movement no longer seems to be part of the young dancer's equipment. Special coaching is going to be required to achieve authentic reconstructions. The same is true with Charles Weidman, who keeps his work alive on a small company of his students, but whose personal range is so reduced now that one can only count on the viewer's imagination to flesh out the movement. Anna Sokolow hasn't had a real dance company for several years, and her works are being done inadequately here and there. With Sokolow the question of expression is supremely important, because her choreography is quite simple. If the dancer cannot find the emotional thrust of the movement—a hand stretching until it topples the whole body, a tiny bounce that expands into a run—Sokolow's work looks like mere histrionics.

Without Martha Graham, the entire contour of contemporary dance, here and abroad, would be different. Besides the possibilities she opened up for expressive movement and subject matter, Graham proved that a

Top: Paul Taylor with his dancers in Aureole
Centre: Three Epitaphs *is a series of zany happenings for five dancers clad all over in black,* *with pieces of mirror glass sewn onto their costume that flash intermittently as the quintet droop and stagger to the sound of primeval jazz*

Left: Paul Taylor and his dancers in Private Domain

Right: Eileen Cropley, Bettie de Jong and Paul Taylor in From Sea to Shining Sea

36

non-balletic dance form can have stature. By her own commanding presence, her rigorous technique and classroom discipline, the consistency and longevity of her company, Graham offered as imposing an image in the world as any ballet organization.

Graham, who is now about 80, returned late in 1972 after a two-year period of illness and dissociation from her work. During that time some of her dancers put together a largely student company as a kind of holding action, and performed works from her repertory in studio conditions. Graham apparently became reconciled during her absence to two great and necessary decisions: she would not perform again and she would help her company reconstruct her old works. The reorganized company's first Broadway season in the spring of 1973 included seven revivals, among them the full-length *Clytemnestra*, plus two new Graham choreographies.

Graham now hopes to bring back a substantial number of the 145 dances she has created since 1926, and to film and notate them as a permanent record. Most Graham revivals in the past have been prepared by former dancers,

without Graham's supervision, and were apt to be re-created for special occasions and quickly dropped again. Not only is it essential to the continuity of American dance that the core of the Graham repertory be accessible to scholars, historians and students in some approximation of their original form; it is important to have real Graham dancing to look at. Graham's dissonant use of the body, her preoccupation with psychological themes, her episodic narrative form have been so thoroughly appropriated and then modified by other choreographers that we have to go back to the source to see her achievement clearly. The American dance world is greatly relieved to see Graham concerned at last with her own posterity.

* * * * *

The other great pioneer in American dance—equal in influence if not in majesty to Graham—is Merce Cunningham. Cunningham didn't invent a new system of dancing so much as change our concept of what dancing can be. His philosophy is one of detachment—he tries to prevent

Previous pages: left: Deuce Coupe by Twyla Tharp

Previous pages: right: John Parkes and Sara Yarborough in Alvin Ailey's Hidden Rites

Top: Mary Hinkson (centre) in Martha Graham's Circe

Right: Martha Graham in Time of Snow

Next pages: Paul Taylor with his dancers in Orbs

all projections of the choreographer's state of mind, politics or sexuality upon the dance. His aesthetic is allied to Cubism: movement need not be linear to make sense. Looking at the landscape of a dance phrase, Cunningham said impulses and follow-throughs need not be side by side; arms need not grow out of a total body line; things can happen in mid-air just as well as on the ground; a literal, "everyday" movement is no less appropriate than a stylized dance movement. This concept was to have enormous importance for a whole generation of post-Cunningham dancers, only a few of whom did anything that looked even remotely like Cunningham.

Cunningham, meanwhile, once we got used to him, began to look more and more balletic. Since he had no particular preference for the expressionistic shapes, off-balances, cleavings to the ground that beguiled other modern dancers, he and his dancers gradually capitulated to their ballet training—the upright, open torso, the meticulous feet and airborne quickness, the emphasis on balancing and proportion.

Few people still regard Cunningham's dances as meaningless or hard to understand. By now he has taught us the value of immediacy, the beauty of chance meetings and partings, the integrity of the unstressed sign. Despite his professed objectivity, many of his dances do have a certain overall feeling—gay or serious, athletic or studious, expansive or closed in—and recently an element of weight has entered his choreography that lends significant personal commitment to the contacts between dancers. *Landrover* (1972), an extraordinary document of the varieties of human touch and support, is, I think, Cunningham's most profoundly moving work.

Cunningham has worked hard to avoid the audience-expansion pressures that have influenced so many other choreographers. He especially likes to perform in non-theatrical spaces, large and small, and to erase the formality of performance-giving by showing dances and parts of dances consecutively, without intermission. Four of his Events were presented to large houses at his spring 1973 Brooklyn Academy season, and the audience didn't understand. Subscribers, many of them, and youngsters attracted by bargain ticket prices, they had no preparation for Cunningham, and they became restless and noisy after an hour or so of nonstop dancing. Cunningham has announced he will disband his company for half a year, ostensibly to investigate film techniques. I suspect, though, that he will also be considering how to bypass the normal touring/prestige theater/mass audience pattern that has been so aggravating to him.

On a more modest, less visible level of activity, New York supports an amazing number of experimental dancers, most of them derived in some way from Cunningham. These might be very grossly sorted out into people who are working with some form of non-dance movement,

Top : Martha Graham as Jocasta in Night Journey

Above : Robert Cohan, now of the London Contemporary Dance Theatre, in Graham's Embattled Garden

Right : Meg Harper and Merce Cunningham in his Rain Forest. *The music was by David Tudor and the decor by Andy Warhol*

Next page : Merce Cunningham's Summerspace

Top : Walkaround Time *by Merce Cunningham*

Above and right : Cunningham and his dancers in *Variations* V. *Barbara Lloyd is seen right. John*

Cage—with whom Cunningham often works—wrote the score

Right : Canfield

48

people inventing new theater-dance forms, people who concentrate on group process and improvisation, and people putting recognizable dance movement into new structures. I can easily list about 45 men and women who have offered very individual conceptions of the dance experience in the last year or two, and only a few of them are following the standard procedure of creating companies, repertories, touring structures, and demonstrable support.

Most of these experimentalists do not seem obsessed with the future. They are not concerned with changing the face of dance; they are more involved in getting their work done. They don't want to refute the past so much as to affirm the present. Most of them don't see themselves as feeding into the establishment or eventually becoming a new establishment; they know there is room for them to exist alongside. Yet Twyla Tharp, the most creative and appealing choreographer to work in ballet for several years, came directly out of this milieu.

Tharp, who danced briefly with Paul Taylor, formed a small company in about 1965. Although they perform infrequently, Tharp's dancers have developed a highly polished and distinctive way of dancing. At first she worked very cerebrally with pure dance movement in complex time and space structures. After a few sorties into museums and outdoor environments, she began choreographing specifically for the stage. Her last four works, *Eight Jelly Rolls, The Bix Pieces, The Raggedy Dances,* and *Deuce Coupe,* have searched deeply into popular music and dance styles—jazz and vaudeville to rock'n'roll—for new sources of energy, new areas of the body that could become added possibilities for the trained modern and ballet dancer.

Tharp is an original in so many ways, but perhaps her most striking and endearing characteristic is her ability to think up grandiose schemes and, with virtually nothing to go on, manage to carry some of them out. Once, for an outdoor dance festival, she wanted to put her company on a barge floating up and down the Hudson River. That didn't work out. Once she organized a second company, which she called the Farm Club, that was supposed to learn and perform her repertory while the main company made new dances. She couldn't pay them anything, but they stayed together for several months. Once she planned a tremendous piece for herself and her five company members and 15 ballet dancers and some teenagers who would paint flamboyant graffiti on the backdrop during the dance. That was *Deuce Coupe.*

The success of *Deuce Coupe* confirms the strength of American dance. Almost as wonderful as the ballet itself is Robert Joffrey's decision to ask Tharp to do it, and the audience's willingness to be captivated by it. A talent like Twyla Tharp's is rare indeed, but it's possible that she could not have occurred in another place.

The Royal Ballet

Above: The corps de ballet in the Kingdom of Shades scene from Petipa's La Bayadère *staged for the Royal Ballet by Rudolf Nureyev—he is seen dancing in the work, right*

Left: Michael Coleman as Solor and Merle Park as Nikiya in La Bayadère

Top right: Dame Margot Fonteyn as Odette with her swan maidens in the fourth act of Swan Lake

Far right: Alfreda Thorogood as Odette; she is one of the new generation of classic ballerinas who now undertake the major roles of the repertory

Previous pages: The Sleeping Beauty *is a ballet particularly associated with the company, and a new staging was mounted in 1973 with Antoinette Sibley as Aurora and Anthony Dowell as Prince Florimund*

Top left: The first appearance of the Wilis in Giselle

Above: Georgina Parkinson as the page-boy in Nijinska's Les Biches, *one of several major ballets of the Diaghilev era which are preserved by the Royal Ballet*

The ballets of Sir Frederick Ashton have been largely responsible for the creation of the English style of classic dancing, and for the development of the Royal Ballet's artists. Ashton's creative range is extraordinarily wide and for nearly 40 years his ballets have given the Royal Ballet much of its identity and present distinction.
Left: Symphonic Variations *was created in 1946, and it has remained in the Royal Ballet repertory ever since as a crucial statement about the classic dance in England. Seen here are David Wall and Laura Connor*

Right: For Fonteyn and Nureyev Ashton created the condensed and ultra-romantic version of La Dame aux Camélias *which he called* Marguerite & Armand

La Fille mal Gardée *has already become immortal, and Ashton's writing for the original quartet of principals—Nadia Nerina as Lise; David Blair as Colas; Alexander Grant as Alain; Stanley Holden as Simone—set new standards for artistry and virtuosity in the Royal Ballet. David Blair is seen top left, and Michael Coleman, one of the Royal Ballet's most dashing virtuosi, is seen left, as Colas in the front-cloth scene, both in Act I*

Above: Monotones One & Two *are a pair of trios to Satie music that Ashton composed in 1965 and 1966. Left are Robert Mead, Vyvyan Lorrayne and Anthony Dowell in* Monotones Two *and right are Georgina Parkinson, Brian Shaw and Antoinette Sibley in* Monotones One

Right: Enigma Variations *was Ashton's evocation of the 'Friends pictured within' by Elgar in his set of orchestral variations. Derek Rencher is Elgar far right, with Svetlana Beriosova as his wife. Alexander Grant is seen right as the boisterous Meath Baker*

Three of Jerome Robbins' ballets have been mounted for the Royal Ballet. Above is the final pose in Robbins' Requiem Canticles. This was first staged as the closing dance work in the New York City Ballet's 1972 Stravinsky Memorial Week, and was then revived for the Royal Ballet later that year. The principals above are Deanne Bergsma, David Ashmole, Wayne Eagling and Vergie Derman; and left is Wayne Eagling, one of the Royal Ballet's brightest young dancers, in the Tuba Mirum solo

Robbins' Dances at a Gathering has been enormously successful: Rudolf Nureyev and Antoinette Sibley are seen in a mazurka, right

The Royal Ballet has paid tribute to the genius of George Balanchine by acquiring six of his ballets that are among the most influential and beautiful of this century. — *Top left:* Four Temperaments *with Deanne Bergsma (centre) as Choleric, and—left to right— Laura Connor, Ria Peri, Ann Jenner and Georgina Parkinson in the final movement*
Far left: Donald MacLeary as Apollo and Svetlana Beriosova as Terpsichore in Balanchine's Apollo
Left: The Prodigal Son *was the last ballet Balanchine made for the Diaghilev company: here David Wall is seen as the Prodigal with Vergie Derman as the Siren*
Above: The Royal Ballet's touring section—the New Group— takes a representative repertory of one-act ballets to towns where the Covent Garden section cannot appear. Les Rendezvous *was Ashton's first work created for the then Vic-Wells Ballet in 1933; here Desmond Kelly is the male dancer with Merle Park*
Right: John Cranko's irresistible Pineapple Poll *has been a delight in the repertory since its creation in 1951. Here Marilyn Trounson is seen as Poll the Midshipman, with part of the would-be crew of HMS Hot Cross Bun*

The Dutch choreographer Hans van Manen has contributed three of his ballets to the New Group's repertory. *Far left:* Twilight *is an aggressive and beautiful pas de deux, danced by Patricia Ruanne and Paul Clarke and below,* Grosse Fuge *with, from left to right, Patricia Ruanne, Carol Hill, Margaret Barbieri and Lois Strike*

Left: The American choreographer and director Herbert Ross' The Maids, *with Kerrison Cooke and Nicholas Johnson*

Right: Glen Tetley has created two major pieces for the Royal Ballet: Field Figures *which was first mounted for the New Group and then taken into the Covent Garden repertory (Rudolf Nureyev is seen right with Monica Mason); and* Laborintus *below with (left) Desmond Kelly, Lynn Seymour and Rudolf Nureyev*

Clement Crisp
Kenneth MacMillan at Work

KENNETH MACMILLAN'S APPOINTMENT AS Director of the Royal Ballet in 1970 marked a vital and essential development in the company's history. Until then the 40 years of our national ballet's existence had been guided by the great talents that originally brought it into being. Dame Ninette de Valois' vision and ideals had created the company and shaped its image; Sir Frederick Ashton's ballets, in conjunction with the 19th-century classic repertory on which de Valois based her company, had formed and polished a clearly English style of dancing. With the coming of MacMillan the company passed on to its second generation.

He came to the post with real experience of the problems, since for three years prior to his appointment he had directed the ballet company of the Deutsche Oper in West Berlin; but his greatest qualification was the fact that he himself was a child of the Royal Ballet. As student, dancer, and as a choreographer who had made 15 ballets for the company, he was heir to its great traditions. His creations were all classic in style, though highlighted with strong dramatic and psychological interest, and it would have been unrealistic not to expect that when he came to direct his parent company, he would seek to extend the range of both ballets and dancers and give each a more modern image. Ballet companies must move forward or they stagnate, and stagnation brings artistic death. Nevertheless, tradition cannot be rejected, and one of the great strengths of the Royal Ballet and the reason for its healthy development has been its solid foundation in the great ballets of the 19th century. It is no mere chance that the most important of these—*The Sleeping Beauty*—has become closely identified with the Royal Ballet both at home and on its triumphant foreign tours. In this ballet in particular the company has shown itself to the world as a great classical troupe, capable of accepting and embellishing the finest achievements of 19th-century dance.

From this background came a native tradition of full-length ballets composed by Ashton: *Cinderella, Sylvia, Ondine, La Fille mal Gardée,* and *The Two Pigeons.* His artistic progeny, John Cranko and Kenneth MacMillan, both imbued with Ashton's understanding of the form and potential of the big ballet, have continued and amplified his revival of the 19th-century formula. After creating the three-act *Prince of the Pagodas* for the Royal Ballet in 1957, Cranko went on to compose a series of full-scale works for his Stuttgart Ballet, as well as restaging *Swan Lake* and *Giselle.* In his turn, MacMillan adopted the form of the big ballet, first with *Romeo and Juliet* in 1965, and, since his return to the Royal Ballet, with *Anastasia* in 1971.

This last work has been both greatly admired and greatly misunderstood. For its devotees it stands as one of the best of MacMillan's ballets (on a par with the glorious *Song of*

Left: Kenneth MacMillan and Brenda Last during a rehearsal of The Poltroon

the Earth), and also as one of the most significant creations of recent years. In Soviet Russia the staging of full-length ballets continued after the Revolution of 1917 and the success of *The Red Poppy* in 1927 revealed that the form and content of the old ballets could be rethought in order to reflect the ideology and special requirements of Soviet aesthetics. Since then, a continuing production of evening-long works has shown considerable vitality, despite the obvious limitations of a directed artistic policy. In recent years two choreographers of the Cranko/MacMillan generation, Yuri Grigorovich and Igor Belsky, have been notably creative, extending their inheritance from the choreographers of the 1930s and 1940s, just as Cranko and MacMillan have in the West. But these Soviet works have all been relevant, in greater or lesser degree, to the actual society being made in Soviet Russia. Outside Soviet Russia, big ballets were still seen in the light of Petipa's grand spectaculars—as splendid and beautiful entertainments, but remote in theme from 20th-century life.

MacMillan's *Anastasia* is a sharp break with the past. Its theme is the amplification of a one-acter he staged in Berlin, a study in the psychology of Anna Anderson, the "Woman Who Believes She Is Anastasia". The original ballet was a searingly effective vehicle for Lynn Seymour, an exploration of the dreams, memories and despair of a woman faced with a crisis of identity. Sure of her own self as sole survivor of the massacre of the Russian imperial family, she is unable to convince the world of this fact. For the Royal Ballet MacMillan decided to give this theme its full historical perspective, to show all the suffering and events that were the fabric of Anna Anderson's tragedy—which would form the final section of a full-length ballet. In this new *Anastasia* we can trace elements that recur in much of MacMillan's creativity: his concern with an isolated "outcast" figure; his interest in the emotional stresses of family relationships; his concern to give vivid physical expression to the inner life of his characters. Yet he was also composing a big work for a big company, in which he must deploy a large number of brilliant soloists—not in the conventional divertissements of the old ballets but in some truer dramatic style.

Act I finds the Russian imperial family picnicking on the Baltic coast during a cruise on the royal yacht; amid all the attendant naval officers and retainers the formalities of court life have been relaxed and the Romanovs are free to be family first and imperial second. The year is 1914, and their happiness seems clouded more by the Tsarevich's ill-health than by the threat of war-clouds. The Tsar's four beautiful daughters sport and play, and the youngest, the Grand Duchess Anastasia, makes her entry on roller skates (just as we see her later, in the final act, where newsreel film of the period shows her skating in the countryside). The lightness of the scene is enhanced by a sequence of brilliant dances for the girls and two trios

The ball at the Capulet's house in Act 1 of Romeo and Juliet *with, top, Lynn Seymour, creator of the role of Juliet; centre, Georgina Parkinson as Juliet in the lute scene and right Lesley Collier as Juliet dancing with Derek Rencher as Paris*

Top left: Monica Mason as the Black Queen in Ninette de Valois' Checkmate

Left: Antoinette Sibley as Titania with a group of fairies in Ashton's The Dream

Above: Dame Margot Fonteyn as Cinderella and David Blair as the Prince; with Alexander Grant as The Jester, and Sir Robert Helpmann and Sir Frederick Ashton as the Ugly Sisters in Ashton's Cinderella

of naval officers, in which virtuoso writing is given real dramatic point; the theme of family relationships, so crucial in the ballet, is shown in the Tsarina's loving dance with her daughters, in the Tsar's delight in photographing his children (another factual touch). Darker undercurrents are hinted at in the vacillating Tsar's dependence on his wife, and in the obvious dominance of Rasputin. The most vivid moment comes when the little Tsarevich falls. The dreadful chill this produces comes from our knowledge that he is haemophiliac, and MacMillan cleverly hints at Rasputin's fatal influence over the Tsarina by showing how he can restore the child to health. As the act ends, a telegram is brought in announcing the mobilization of Germany and the onset of the First World War; the German-born Tsarina and her daughters watch aghast as the Tsar and his officers leave. History has been treated freely, poetically, but the vital facts of an actual situation—the Tsar's weakness, his reliance upon his wife, Rasputin's malign dominion over the Tsarina—have all been stated.

Important in understanding both this act and the succeeding one is the ballet's title. The Grand Duchess Anastasia is the central figure; we are, in a sense, seeing the world through her eyes. Her feelings for her family, her youthful incomprehensions, are the ballet's viewpoint, and they are to return and be amplified in the last act.

In Act I MacMillan has brought off a notable exercise in style and period evocation; brilliant and beautiful dances abound, but within a clear emotional and historical framework. His use of Tchaikovsky's First Symphony is skilful; only in the closing fugal section of the last movement—impossible to cut effectively on musical grounds—does the action seem overextended in the marching and countermarching of the naval officers.

In Act I Anastasia is still a child; Act II, which takes place in Petrograd in the early spring of 1917, finds her a girl on the brink of womanhood. Here MacMillan has had to take some historical liberties in order to arrive at the truth about his central character. A frontcloth scene takes place in a bitterly cold street, where a soup-kitchen feeds the starving masses and a wounded soldier is dragged past as a reminder of the appalling defeats that have beset the Russian armies. Tchaikovsky's Third Symphony is the score here; after this dark opening page, we are transported into the glittering splendour of a court ball in the Winter Palace, given by Nicholas II to celebrate Anastasia's coming of age. In the enclosed world of the palace all is superficially serene; gorgeously clothed guests dance and watch a divertissement performed by the *prima ballerina assoluta* of the Imperial Ballet, Mathilda Kshessinskaya (one time mistress of the Tsar), and her partner. MacMillan brings off a magnificent feat of con-

Above: Lynn Seymour as the Eldest Sister, with Gerd Larsen (behind) as the Mother, and Margaret Barbieri as the Youngest Sister (second from right) in Las

Hermanas, *as staged by the Royal Ballet's New Group. The ballet is based upon Frederico Garcia Lorca's play* The House of Bernarda Alba

Top right: Monica Mason as the Chosen Maiden in The Rite of Spring *dancing the dance of exhaustion which causes the Maiden's death and fulfills the Rite*

Opposite left: Brenda Last as Columbine and Donald MacLeary as Pierrot in The Poltroon *written for the Royal Ballet's New Group Far right: The quartet of friends*

68

struction here by fitting a virtuoso *pas de deux* for them to the *alla tedesca* of the symphony. There follows a scene in which Anastasia, still uncomprehending of the emotional complexities of her parents' life, watches them as they become involved with Rasputin and Kshessinskaya. The presence of these two characters is historically inadmissible, but complete verisimilitude is not the function of a ballet, and through this sequence MacMillan arrives at illuminating insights into his characters. We move briefly from the ballroom back into the street to witness the first rumblings of revolutionary fervour, and when the scene changes back to the ballroom the sweeping and splendid inventions of a Polonaise for the court are interrupted finally and inevitably by the irruption of the revolutionaries, who set about massacring the guests and tearing down the decorations. The final act—the original Berlin *Anastasia*—comes as a deliberate artistic shock. The period is the 1920s, the world of Tsarist Russia has been swept away. Gone are the opulent costumes; gone, too, is the magic of Tchaikovsky—the score is now Martinú's Symphonic Fantasy. We are in a Berlin hospital where "The Woman Who Believes She Is Anastasia", crop-haired and in a functional blue dress, is the focal point for a whirlwind of images, memories, nightmares. Desperately trying to remember who she is, she relives fragments of her childhood (film projection show us the

real imperial family with the recurrent figure of a solemn-eyed Anastasia), the massacre in the Ekaterinburg cellar, her rescue, marriage and the birth of her child who is cruelly taken from her, and her rejection by the surviving relatives of the Romanovs. Personalities and incidents become confused and elided: Anna Anderson finds herself trapped in a labyrinth of distorting mirrors which throw back at her twisted and mocking reflections of her lost life. Her family reappears, at first like ghosts, then more real than the new world in which she finds herself. All she has to sustain her is one fact: her own belief in herself as Anastasia, and at the last, in a supreme effort of will, she defies the world, circling the stage on her bed, certain of her own identity.

Anastasia is an important, beautiful and innovative work of art. With it MacMillan has developed the capabilities of the three-act ballet, and for the first time in the West a big ballet has escaped from the usual restrictions of its form to find in recent history a theme that admits of lengthy treatment, transmuting history's truth into a no less truthful poetry. It is a ballet which offers tremendous challenges to its casts—notably to Lynn Seymour, whose creation of the central role was in every way marvellous—and it is a remarkable justification of the *ballet à grand spectacle* today as a valid means of artistic expression.

The other ballets that MacMillan has created during the

in Ballade, *written by MacMillan for the Royal Ballet's New Group: Kerrison Cooke and Vyvyan Lorrayne, with Stephen Jeffries and Nicholas Johnson*

Over top: Svetlana Beriosova as the Bride in the first scene of Nijinska's Les Noces *and below left with Donald MacLeary in* Cinderella, *Act II. Below right:*

Margot Fonteyn and Rudolf Nureyev in Roland Petit's Paradise Lost. *Far right: Merle Park as The Celestial and Anthony Dowell as The Boy with Matted*

Hair, in Antony Tudor's Shadow-play

years of his directorate are all small-scale pieces. The first was *Checkpoint* (1970), in which a bold theatrical idea went sadly wrong. Inspired by a passage in George Orwell's *1984*, it was an extended *pas de deux* for two lovers trapped in a police state of the future, whose desire to express their love and whose very individuality were crushed by the forces of Big Brother. But the initial conception failed to inspire choreography of any urgency, and the work was swiftly abandoned. There followed *Anastasia,* and then *Triad* (1972) set to Prokofiev's Violin Concerto no. 1 in which MacMillan's recurrent concern with the intricacies and tensions of family relationships found a subject and interpreters that inspired some exceptional dances. We were shown how the companionship between two brothers was destroyed when the elder first fell in love with a girl. The ballet's sympathies are with the younger brother, and his suffering and jealousy are the focal point of the action. The role was created for Wayne Eagling, a brilliant young classical soloist, and one of MacMillan's most distinctive gifts—his ability to reveal the innermost feeling of a character in burningly clear movement—was fully deployed here, as in

Anastasia. Top left: The Tsarina Alexandra (Svetlana Beriosova) with three of her daughters: top right: Antoinette Sibley as Kshessinskaya, with her partner, *Anthony Dowell: right: Lynn Seymour as The Grand Duchess Anastasia in Act II, and left, as the woman who thinks she is Anastasia in Act III*

a passage when the boy's confusion of spirit is pinpointed in an extraordinary curving circuit of the stage in which he spins and turns and sinks to the floor. The role of the elder brother was composed for Anthony Dowell, and his impeccable classic style was given an added sharpness and brilliance of outline that suggested a great deal about the youth's temperament and developing maturity. *Ballade* followed in the same year, a light-textured and atmospheric work made for the dancers of the Royal Ballet's New Group (the section of the company that undertakes most of its touring commitments in Britain). The ballet is a brief incident concerned with the fluid interchange of relationships between a girl and her three man friends. Basically about the awakening of love, it is delicate and understated; the four characters find that their common friendship is disturbed when one boy falls in love with the girl, and the happiness of this new relationship is countered by the comments and responses of the two other boys, who question and test the new balance that now exists between them all. In no sense an important work, *Ballade* (which used Fauré's Ballade for piano as its accompaniment) depended upon a fluent, "open" style of writing and extremely intricate partnering to obtain its effects.

MacMillan also made another ballet for the New Group in 1972: *The Poltroon*. This work marked an interesting change in his treatment of a type that has been central to much of his creativity: the "outcast figure", the character

forced into isolation by circumstances or society. In *The Poltroon* the outcast bursts from his isolation, the worm turns: in the words of the programme note "he faces his persecutors, and looks in the yellow of their eyes with dramatic results". The setting is a *commedia dell'arte* troupe, a hectic, vulgar assembly of traditional figures, nasty one and all, save for their victim, Pierrot. They mock and deride him, especially in his idealism and his illusory love for a sluttish Columbine. After a violent amorous bout with her, Pierrot strangles her: the dreamer has awakened, the introvert has distilled a vicious strength from his suffering, and in an access of frenzy in which his whole personality is turned inside out, he kills all his tormentors. The ballet is a work of almost feverish theatricality, deliberately lurid in its tone. It was not entirely successful —the Rudolf Maros score proved too long, and MacMillan had to pad some of the dances (he works best in dramatic pieces when he has to concentrate his effects, as in the masterly *Las Hermanas*). Nevertheless, *The Poltroon* was still a bold work, and it inspired sharp, biting characterizations from its cast.

Quite as indicative of his aims as his own ballets are the works that have been staged for the Royal Ballet since MacMillan became its director. These suggest a continuing concern for an expansion of experience for the company and its individual dancers. This is typified by the acquisition of works from Jerome Robbins and Glen Tetley. Since 1970 three Robbins ballets have entered the

Previous pages: left Antoinette Sibley and Anthony Dowell in the balcony scene from Romeo and Juliet

Previous pages: right Lynn Seymour as the young Grand Duchess Anastasia in Act I of Anastasia

Above: Wayne Eagling and Anthony Dowell as the two brothers in Triad, *with Antoinette Sibley as the girl*

Top right: Lynn Seymour and Rudolf Nureyev in Sideshow, *a comedy duet by MacMillan, in which they play a strong-man and an equestrienne who find themselves*

repertory: *Dances at a Gathering, Afternoon of a Faun*, and *Requiem Canticles*. The joyous, exhilarating *Dances* is a hymn to the pleasures and splendours of the *danse d'école*; *Faun* shows how an old ballet (Nijinsky's original dated from 1912) can be rethought for modern audiences; *Canticles* is a succinct and datingly novel expression of the themes and attitudes of Stravinsky's last major composition—what the composer himself called "a celebration of death".

The two Tetley ballets—*Field Figures* and *Laborintus*—are the most adventurous and forward-looking works ever staged by the Royal Ballet. Tetley, an American choreographer who has worked largely in Europe, was trained in what have customarily been thought the conflicting disciplines of classical ballet and modern dance. Out of this experience he has forged a style that combines the two in a very personal and expressive language.

The Royal Ballet's dancers rose magnificently to the very real challenge of Tetley's uniquely individual style, revealing the same skill and distinction that they show in their classic repertory. It is in works like those of Robbins and Tetley, quite as much as MacMillan's own ballets or in the continued preservation of the great works of the past from the era of Petipa and Fokine to that of Ashton, that the Royal Ballet's identity can best be seen today. The company is becoming more flexible in manner under MacMillan; although soundly rooted in the greatest achievements of the past, and sustained by the classic repertory and by a classic school, the company still must look for new means of expression. Awareness of the future seems to me to be one of the keynotes of MacMillan's directorship as well as of his creativity; but any development must be logical and organic. There has been no abrupt change of style or image; the company will always remain a classic troupe. Yet classicism itself is constantly developing—therein lies its great strength. MacMillan's taste and the fact of his own artistic formation by the company he now directs will show just how fruitful such a development can be.

in wild and unpredictable troubles Right: Antoinette Sibley and Anthony Dowell in Pavane, *the duet to Fauré's Pavane which MacMillan wrote for them on the occasion of the Covent Garden Fanfare for Europe Gala in 1973 Over top left: Anastasia at her coming-out ball in* Anastasia, *Act II, with Carl Myers, Lesley Collier, and Michael Coleman. Over below left: Rudolf Nureyev*

warming up at a make-shift barre before a television performance of the Romeo and Juliet *balcony pas de deux Over top right: The closing scene of* The Three-Cornered Hat, *performed by Festival Ballet. Leonide Massine's magnificent evocation of Spain, is the only truly successful Spanish ballet. Here the villagers are seen celebrating the discomfiture of the*

hated Corregidor as they toss him sky-high in effigy. Sets and costumes by Picasso are among the the most brilliant ever produced by the Diaghilev Ballet.

Over below right: Galina Samtsova and André Prokovsky in The Sleeping Beauty *as staged by London Festival Ballet.*

London
Festival
Ballet

London Festival Ballet will soon be 25 years old. The company has spent its near quarter of a century touring far and wide with stagings of the classics, revivals of some of Mikhail Fokine's early works for Diaghilev, a broad selection of popular one-act ballets, and special creations for the company.

Left: Galina Samtsova was born and trained in Russia, and her expansive and brilliant style has earned her tremendous acclaim throughout the world

Top: Galina Samtsova and André Prokovsky as Kitri and Basil in Don Quixote

Above: Dagmar Kessler is held by Peter Schaufuss in the famous "fish dives" of the pas de deux in the final act of Sleeping Beauty

Top right: Galina Samtsova and Robert Bestonso as two moths, and André Prokovsky as a convict in John Taras's Piège de Lumière,

a poetic work about escaped convicts in the South American jungle who live by trapping moths and selling them

George Balanchine's Night Shadow *is a high-romantic story of a poet who meets and falls in love with a somnambulist.*

Centre: Galina Samtsova as the sleep-walker with Alain Dubreuil as the poet

Right: Maria Guerrero, Dudley von Loggenburg and Gaye Fulton in the pas de trois from Act I of the recent production of Swan Lake *by Beryl Grey*

Barry Moreland, a young Australian choreographer, came to London as a dancer and made his first ballets for the London Contemporary Dance Company at The Place. He then joined Festival Ballet as choreographer and dancer and two works illustrated here show something of his range as a creator. *Left:* Dudley von Loggenburg and Gaye Fulton in Summer Solstice; *on page 84, a scene from a religious work,* In Nomine, *with Alain Dubreuil*

Left: Peter Schaufuss is the son of two celebrated Danish dancers, Frank Schaufuss and Mona Vangsaa, and Mme Vangsaa supervised a revival of some dances from Bournonville's Napoli, one of the greatest treasures of the Danish repertory, for Festival Ballet. Peter Schaufuss is shown here in one of the characteristically bounding Bournonville jumps

Top right: Petrushka, *Fokine's masterpiece, has long featured in Festival Ballet's repertory. The scene is set in 1840, and the dolls—Blackamoor (Dudley von Loggenburg), Ballerina (Galina Samtsova) and the tragic Petrushka (André Prokovsky) are just being summoned to life by the old Charlatan*

Centre: Festival Ballet's artists at the beginning of Harold Lander's Études, *while the dancers are still demonstrating barre exercises*

Right: Festival Ballet in Dvořák Variations, *a work created for the company by Ronald Hynd*

Scottish Theatre Ballet

For a decade Western Theatre Ballet was one of the most enterprising dance companies in Britain, with a repertory that insisted quite as much upon the "theatre" in the company's titles as on the "ballet". Directed first by Elizabeth West, and then by Peter Darrell, following her tragic death, the company attracted an ever increasing audience and won artistic fame. In 1969 the company moved north in compliance with a policy to encourage regionalism in the arts, and established itself in Glasgow as the Scottish Theatre Ballet. Since then the company has developed, staging new full-length ballets, and also classic works, while continuing its policy of experimental creativity with remarkable success.

Previous page: Marian St Claire and Kenn Wells in Peter Darrell's second full-length ballet, Beauty and the Beast

Top left: Gernot Petzold and Elaine McDonald in Peter Darrell's Tales of Hoffmann

Centre left: La Fête Étrange, *a revival of Andrée Howard's ballet, with (left to right) Harold King, Terence James, Amanda Oliver*

Top: Anthony Pannell and Bruce Stievel in Toer van Schayk's Ways of Saying Bye-bye

Above: The Queen of the Wilis dismisses Hilarion to his doom: a scene from Peter Darrell's new staging of Giselle *for Scottish Theatre Ballet*

Left: Walter Gore's Street Games

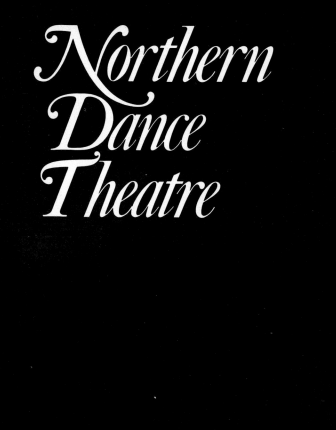

Northern
Dance
Theatre

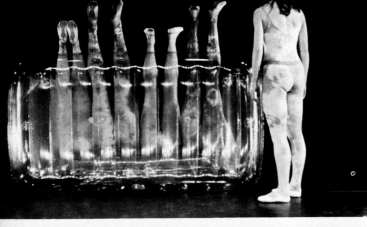

The development of regional ballet in Britain has been slow, but the concept of establishing local troupes in the provinces has now been accepted in favour of the big organizations touring the country at infrequent intervals. The successful transfer of Western Theatre Ballet from the south to a permanent home in Glasgow was an indication of the opportunities that existed, and a former Western Theatre Ballet dancer and choreographer, Laverne Meyer, decided to form a company to be based in Manchester. From its inception in November 1969 Northern Dance Theatre has laboured hard to put down roots in its chosen region, and show audiences that ballet does not necessarily mean a large company and an eternity of *Swan Lake*, but that ingenuity and a concern to foster talent will bring real and lasting rewards.

Top left: Northern Dance Theatre has revived several works originally created for other companies which might otherwise have been lost. Here the dancers are seen in Frank Staff's Peter and the Wolf

Centre: John Chesworth's Games for Five Players *is about the games people play and involves inflatable plastic furniture*

Left: The Wanderer and his Shadow *with John Fletcher held by Peter Kyle; a ballet staged by Jonathan Thorpe, a dancer with NDT*

Northern Dance Theatre invited the distinguished choreographer, Walter Gore, to mount several works, and invited Gore's wife, Paula Hinton, as guest. Hinton is an artist of unique dramatic and expressive gifts and is seen on the previous page as the Woman in Night and Silence

Above: Laverne Meyer's three-act Cinderella *was an ambitious undertaking for the young company and proved a mild and domestic retelling of the tale: Carol Barrett as Cinderella*

John Percival
Dance at
The Place

Y OU WILL NOT FIND ROBIN HOWARD'S name listed on the programmes of The Place, the theatre he founded in a former army drill hall behind St Pancras Church at Euston, nor among the staff of The London Contemporary Dance Theatre, which has its home there. Yet without him, neither of these would have come into existence, nor have survived the crises which beset any young pioneering venture in the arts. He has an astonishing gift for making improbable things happen; largely, I suspect, because he somehow makes his wildest dreams seem quietly reasonable. A big, gentle man, badly injured during the Second World War, he is both modest and shy, but full of a generous enthusiasm that inspires other people with his own ideals and confidence.

He has been interested in dancing, off and on, since childhood. First, as a boy in Scotland, it was Highland dancing; later, in the days after the war, classical ballet. But by 1954 he had grown dissatisfied with what he was seeing, and found himself attending fewer performances. In that year a friend persuaded him to go to see the American dancer Martha Graham, who was playing in London to disastrously small but wildly enthusiastic houses. (One night there were only 30 people in the auditorium, but they stayed to cheer at the end.) Robin Howard went, and was completely bowled over by Graham's distinctive style of dancing and choreography, which seemed to him to embody a "deep intellectual and psychological truth in harmony with aesthetic truth". He sent her the first fan letter he had ever written, met her before she returned to New York . . . and there it might all have ended.

A few years later, returning from a spell of working abroad, Robin Howard heard that Martha Graham was touring Europe but not coming to London. "I asked the silly question, why not, and got the obvious answer that there was no fool prepared to lose a lot of money on it." He decided to play the fool himself, together with some of his friends. With their backing Graham came to London, and danced every night to a sold-out house.

This time it was not only Robin Howard who was bowled over. Innumerable dancers said they wanted to study the system of "contemporary dance" which Graham had evolved for herself. A lecture demonstration of her theories and technique was packed, with people standing at the back of the theatre. Britain, until then supremely uninterested in anything except the pure classical ballet, had suddenly discovered the modern dance that had long flourished in the United States.

Actually there had been earlier attempts to establish modern dance here. Way back in the early days of the movement, the pioneers had performed in London, but the British public seemed to prefer the genteel Maud Allen to the genuinely revolutionary Isadora Duncan. Later, to our credit, we provided a home for Kurt Jooss after his radical views forced him to leave Germany, but several different attempts to build a recognizably English modern dance group all failed for lack of talent. While so much effort was going into establishing classical ballet in England, this was understandable, but with the acceptance of the Royal Ballet as one of the world's great companies, the time had come when there was room for a genuine opposition movement.

Martha Graham's visit to London was followed by seasons in which several of America's other leading modern dancers appeared: Merce Cunningham, Paul Taylor, Alvin Ailey. Enthusiasm mounted, and one evening Robin Howard invited all the London dance critics to a meal at a dining club he then owned on a boat on the River Thames. (He had made his living as a very successful restaurateur, running a series of hotels, restaurants and clubs.) His purpose was not purely social, but an attempt to ensure that the effect of these successive seasons was preserved.

Characteristically, he produced a long, detailed and logically argued account of exactly what he wanted to achieve and how he proposed to attempt it. Characteristically too, he then offered to change any part of it if others had better suggestions to make. It is evidence of his foresight that the programme has developed almost exactly as he then outlined it.

Previous page: Linda Gibbs in Talley Beatty's The Road of the Phoebe Snow, *a work about the railways and slum areas of the Chicago stockyards*

Left: in Martha Graham's El Penitente *Robert Cohan is seen left as The Penitent, with Noemi Lapzeson as the Magdalen*

The first step was to set up a trust fund to which he persuaded many of his business friends, as well as many lovers of dancing, to contribute, although it is an open secret that a great part of the money came from his own pocket. Next, selected British dancers were sent to study in New York, and teachers from America were imported to London. Within two years a full-time school of contemporary dance was open in London, with Martha Graham as artistic adviser and one of her partners, Robert Cohan, as director. Before the first full academic year was over, the pupils were already rehearsing for their first appearance as a company in a week of performances in the Adeline Genée Theatre at East Grinstead in Sussex (carefully selected so that they would not, at this initial tryout, be judged by London standards).

Telling it like this makes the whole affair sound too easy. In fact the fate of the enterprise has been almost always poised on a knife's edge throughout its history. To give just one instance, there came the time when the rapidly expanding school, which had been started in temporary premises, needed quickly to move into a suitable long-term home. In his search, Robin Howard came across the empty building that had formerly been the headquarters of the volunteer regiment known as the Artists' Rifles. It was ideal for his purpose, but there was just one difficulty: money.

Robin Howard, once a wealthy man, had spent almost all his own money and whatever he could raise from sympathizers. He had asked the Arts Council for help and met with encouraging words, but only very limited funds because of other commitments. In fact, the whole venture was facing bankruptcy.

The sensible course was to retract, but then the initiative might never have been regained. Robin Howard decided to take a calculated risk. Instead of cutting back expenditure, he pressed on even faster with his long-term plans. A lease was taken on the building and an architect engaged to convert it, providing a theatre, studios, offices, a box office, changing rooms, storage space and a canteen. The aim was, by risking all the resources available, to start earning income that would enable everything to keep going; and it worked. At Easter 1969 the London School of Contemporary Dance moved in. That summer the first experimental public events were held, and in September the premises were officially declared open by Lord Goodman, chairman of the Arts Council, on the opening night of the first London season of the company which Robin Howard and Robert Cohan had formed—the London Contemporary Dance Theatre.

The original idea had been to call the building Artists' Place, a name appropriate to both its old and its new owners, but this was shortened to The Place on the grounds that people would abbreviate the name anyway and also that it sounded more friendly. The dance com-

Top right: Robert North in his ballet Brian, *a tragedy about a schizophrenic boy, seen here with Linda Gibbs, and—in the background—Stephen Barker*

Right: William Louther as the Hero in Robert Cohan's Stages, *with members of the London Contemporary Dance Company as the creatures who torment him*

pany and the school have always had to share it with other organizations, partly through sheer economic need, partly because there was always the wish to prevent any danger of the students becoming interested only in dance to the exclusion of other things. Classical ballet classes, musical groups, including the Pierrot Players and the experimental Music Now, two cinema clubs and Geoff Moore's mixed-media group Moving Being are among the many enterprises which have made their home at The Place from time to time, and the main entrance hall is generally used for art exhibitions.

Flexibility has been the keynote all along. The first performances at The Place were called Explorations and at once set the tone for all the out of the ordinary activities which have followed. Different artists and groups were invited to try out any ideas they liked almost anywhere in the building. Alan Beattie involved both dancers and spectators with coloured lights and PVC sheeting in a "Green Maze" in the entrance hall. Upstairs, Art Bauman from New York mingled dancers and films, while in the

basement a young sculptor, Peter Logan, set up a mysterious corridor with moving ribbons, monsters, and a human leg projecting through one wall.

Most activities, however, naturally take place in the theatre which is the heart of the building. It holds about 300 spectators and the seating is completely flexible, so that producers have a choice of a conventional proscenium stage, an open stage, theatre in the round, thrust stage, or whatever variant they fancy.

Drama companies—including the Royal Shakespeare Company for one of their experimental seasons—have been glad to appear there, but the prime value of The Place is that it gives London for the first time a theatre that is intended for dance companies. Classical ballet does not look good in this informal setting, with the audience close to the dancers, as the Northern Dance Theatre from Manchester discovered in its first London season, but more experimental companies from Argentina, France, Holland, Israel, Sweden and the United States have played there, generally with success. Some of them would

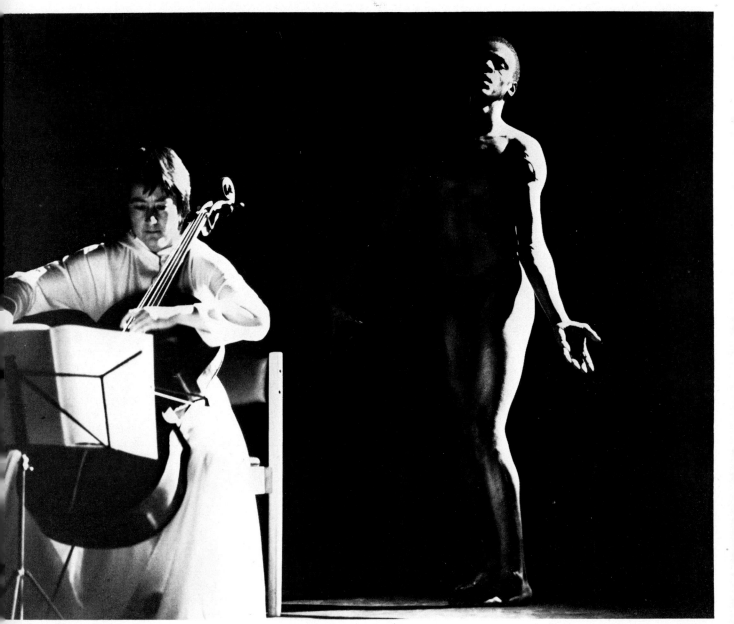

not have danced in London at all had this theatre not been available, with its reputation for an open-minded policy and its regular audience of young enthusiasts.

Naturally, the company most often seen at The Place is the resident London Contemporary Dance Theatre, which generally has about three seasons there each year. Between these, the company undertakes a certain amount of touring and also devotes much time to preparing a constant flow of new works.

Surprisingly, since Martha Graham provided the original inspiration for the venture and gave it her blessing and support, only one of her ballets has been included in the repertory. This was her early work *El Penitente*, about a group of strolling players presenting the story of Christ, which was danced at the company's London debut by Cohan with two other American stars, Noemi Lapzeson and William Louther. Cohan would have been glad to mount one or two other works by Graham, but practical considerations have made this impossible. Besides, the intention was from the first that the company should

present mainly new ballets specially made for its own dancers, and largely in fact created by them.

Other guest choreographers, mostly American, have mounted works for the company. Paul Taylor's beautiful *Duet* and his comic *Three Epitaphs* have particularly enriched the repertory, as did Alvin Ailey's touching *Hermit Songs*. These were all for small casts of soloists, but Talley Beatty's dramatic jazz ballet *The Road of the Phoebe Snow* and Anna Sokolow's *Scenes from the Music of Charles Ives* each involved the whole company.

The most prolific of the company's own choreographers is Robert Cohan. His most striking work so far is *Cell*, an enigmatic but grippingly claustrophobic dance drama for six characters in a labyrinthine setting by Norberto Chiesa, with an impressive central role which was first danced by a guest from the Graham company, Robert Powell. Cohan also produced with much success *Stages*, a spectacular work in two acts incorporating athletics, trick lighting, elaborate stage effects, films and a part electronic, part jazz score. Another particularly distinguished

creation for the company was *Vesalii Icones*, a collaboration between the dancer William Louther and the composer Peter Maxwell Davies, based on medieval anatomical drawings and the Stations of the Cross.

A feature of the training at the London School of Contemporary Dance is that all the students are required to create dances as part of their courses. Because of this, a great many of the dancers in the company have staged works for the repertory. Many have shown promise, but the one who so far has achieved more than any of the others is Richard Alston. Still in his early twenties, he began to study dance after leaving Eton, and though he proved unsuited for a career as a dancer, he showed an ability to absorb many different styles and make something individual out of them. His musical inspiration has ranged from the avant-garde John Cage (*Night Music*) to blues, jazz and pop. In the autumn of 1972 Alston formed his own group, Strider, to present a repertory of works by himself and some of the other dancers, with the particular intention of working in colleges and thus laying the group open to influences from other arts.

This departure might have been expected to weaken the company, but fortunately it occurred just at a time when reinforcements of new talent (both creative and performing) were coming from the school, some of them graduating through an intermediate organization, the London Contemporary X Group, which experiments with new works, appears in places that are too small for the main company, and gives experience to young dancers.

Alston's group represents a breakaway, but not a complete break. Their rehearsals were held at The Place, and they made their debut there. Robin Howard drew up their initial budget and nominated them for a grant from the Gulbenkian Foundation's dance awards fund. On their first night he told me, "You know, this is really the moment I have been looking forward to—when some of the people we have trained would turn round and say 'We don't agree with the way you are doing things, we want to do it our own way.'"

Although Martha Graham provided the initial inspiration, two decades ago, and although most of the first teachers, choreographers and stars were inevitably borrowed from America, the aim has always been to build a genuinely British company. Now the seeds of hope which Robin Howard planted are beginning to blossom in their new soil.

Left: William Louther in the solo Hermit Songs *created for him by the American choreographer Alvin Ailey*

Previous pages: left William Louther (with the 'cellist Jennifer Ward Clark) in Vesalii Icones, *a work he created in collaboration with the composer Peter Maxwell Davies. It is designed to draw a parallel between the anatomical drawings of Andreas Vesalius (published in 1543) and the Stations of the Cross. Louther, a dancer of superlative gifts, gave a performance of unforgettable dignity and beauty in this work—*
—as in many others
Right: Cold, *by Richard Alston, is a playful Modern Dance commentary upon one of classical ballet's sacred texts, the second act of* Giselle. *Alston is one of many talented and original creators produced by the London School of Contemporary Dance*

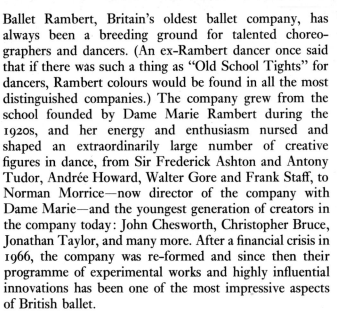

Ballet Rambert, Britain's oldest ballet company, has always been a breeding ground for talented choreographers and dancers. (An ex-Rambert dancer once said that if there was such a thing as "Old School Tights" for dancers, Rambert colours would be found in all the most distinguished companies.) The company grew from the school founded by Dame Marie Rambert during the 1920s, and her energy and enthusiasm nursed and shaped an extraordinarily large number of creative figures in dance, from Sir Frederick Ashton and Antony Tudor, Andrée Howard, Walter Gore and Frank Staff, to Norman Morrice—now director of the company with Dame Marie—and the youngest generation of creators in the company today: John Chesworth, Christopher Bruce, Jonathan Taylor, and many more. After a financial crisis in 1966, the company was re-formed and since then their programme of experimental works and highly influential innovations has been one of the most impressive aspects of British ballet.

Top left: Norman Morrice's 1-2-3 dealt with the awakening feelings—both happy and unhappy—between two men and a woman, and it treated a theme Morrice was to return to later in Hazard
Centre: Norman Morrice's That is the Show *was inspired by the text and score of Luciano Berio's Sinfonia. Morrice gives it no explicit theme, preferring his audience to interpret and understand the ballet as they wish. What is important is the skill and beauty of the choreography and the excellence of the dance performances which have made this a major British ballet*
Left: One of the happiest new developments by the Ballet Rambert is the children's show Bertram Batell's Circus (an anagram not difficult to solve), in which Bertram himself (in the centre of picture) is guide and compère to a series of dance scenes made by members of the company. These can be jolly, serious, or just plain skittish, and all are adored by a young audience who learn to understand and love ballet the easy way

Previous page: Tetley's first creation for Ballet Rambert was Ziggurat, a densely-written and beautiful exploration of man in relationship with his gods: Dreas Reyneke and Paul Taras

Top right: A scene from Norman Morrice's Blind-sight, a study in intolerance and mass cruelty, with Jonathan Taylor
Far right: A scene from Hazard, one of Norman Morrice's best works which dealt with the tragedies brought about by sexual rivalries within a group. Christopher Bruce is the dancer
Right: Christopher Bruce, a principal of the company, made his sixth ballet, There was a Time, for a thrust stage. It is a comment upon the nature of war as seen in the Trojan conflict. The warriors fight: a slow-motion combat of extraordinary power

Above: Scottish Theatre Ballet with Kenn Wells and Patricia Rianne in Bournonville's La Ventana

Johann Meyer in Louis Falco's Huescape *performed by the Nederlands Dans Theater*

Robert Cohan's Mass *performed by the London Contemporary Dance Theatre*

Maurice Béjart
Dynamic Tradition

DANCE PLAYED A LARGE PART IN THE LIFE of primitive man, who, while neither better nor worse than we, certainly allotted much more importance to intuition. Dance is an essentially intuitive art and to me intuition is the human being's sense of his place within the universe, which is nearly always found to perfection among primitive peoples. The importance of dance in today's world is as a major means of communication. It re-creates all that this century tends to destroy. As I have said many times, dance has its roots in both the sacred and the social, and all dance that does not incorporate these, even unconsciously, is ineffectual because it is deprived of its origins. What is more, both these origins are to be found in all countries that have retained a folk tradition. That is why, in India, sacred dancing is part of the religious tradition, and is taught in the temples, whereas popular dancing is integrated into village life and can be seen in public places.

This is not the case in the West, for the simple reason that at a time when sacred art was part of the Church, the sole centre of spiritual and artistic inspiration, dance was systematically alienated. In those days, the Church permitted music, painting, sculpture—but it did not like dance, which therefore never evolved, either as an art form or as a part of daily life.

At the present time in the West, the meaing of this art has been lost; hence classical dance has become the art of making people dance who do not do so naturally, with the help of a mathematical vocabulary that tries to mitigate the deficiencies of a body that has really long since been dead. To me, dance represents life—and because life is a rhythm, that of the heartbeat—dance is inseparable from rhythm. It interprets our existence, to the extent that it represents all the rhythms, all the human pulsations.

To my mind there probably is no ideal dancer, because the art of dance varies from day to day. No dancer can ever claim to be perfect, and each time he practises at the bar he has to wrestle anew with his muscles, with his whole body, his pride, his will. There is a new achievement in each day. To me, the ideal dancer would be the one who could end up by thinking with his whole body. In 20th-century ballet, work starts with the muscles and continues with the brain—the personality of the dancer always has a determining role. A good dancer must therefore have a perfect technique, but he must also have the power to forget about it, or better still make others forget about it, while he is dancing.

It has sometimes been said that dancers are not very intelligent. In fact, that could become a compliment. I think that people these days live too much in their heads and not enough in their legs. The human body makes fewer mistakes than the brain. What I most admire in dancers is their superb physical condition. When one sweats, one isn't making any mistakes! An equilibrium can be achieved, but it is hard for us because our civilization has learned to put too much emphasis on the head's contribution and not enough on the legs'. One can tell lies with words, and with notes, but the body never lies.

I think it was Gustav Mahler who said that "tradition is letting things take their course," and, indeed, very often when people use the word "tradition" they are inviting laziness. They take refuge behind a ready-made notion which is actually the opposite of tradition. To me, tradition is a river, a movement, an action, a wish to go from one place to another. The music of Beethoven is traditional now, yet Beethoven himself was a revolutionary in his own time. I think that tradition should continue the flow of a particular artistic direction; it is a question of knowing the message of the past, of being able to appreciate it and to reconstruct it in terms of the present. Tradition is more than anything a dynamic element, which is all too often betrayed by the very people who invoke it and thereby confuse tradition and convention, laziness and respect, lack of imagination and good taste.

I have sometimes been asked whether one needs a story or an anecdote on which to build a ballet. Dance itself can do without anecdotes, but there is a difference between dance and ballet. Dance is pure art in itself, while ballet is dance in the service of the universe. There is the same distinction between music and opera. If you compose a symphony, you are creating pure music, whereas if you write an opera, you are using music to express a dramatic purpose. Ballet is to dance what opera is to music. If I create an abstract dance lasting 15 minutes or half an hour, I achieve a symphony in movements which says nothing specific but which expresses a general idea or an emotion. By contrast, *Romeo and Juliet*, which tells a specific story, is a ballet.

It is interesting that in passing through the act of creation, a work is always transformed. When a film director takes a celebrated novel and brings it to the screen, he transforms the novel. There is always an adaptation and a re-creation which is stimulated by the impression the work itself has made on the director or choreographer. I keep coming back to the difference between pure music and dramatic music. If I take a symphony, like Beethoven's Ninth, for instance, or a work of Xenakis, or Boulez, I find myself in the presence of pure music, and I respect that music. Such music is an object in itself, of which I would not touch a note. When I choose some dramatic music, however, I allow myself the right to revise it completely. When Berlioz used Goethe's *Faust*, he adapted and completely changed the original work. In the same way, if I create a dramatic ballet, such as *Romeo and Juliet*, I change the music completely.

Percussion plays an important part in my musical accompaniments because it is the basis of dance. Dance is a rhythm which needs support. The line of an arm is a melodic line, while the movement of the heart is percussive. Percussion is ideal for sustaining the dance without adding any other melody to that of the human body.

I don't really plan a work; it is more a question of following the changes of our civilization, of living through them, and of deducing constantly the kind of moving spectacle that will serve as their reflection. I try to place question marks in order to wake up the spectators, and make them question their own behaviour. *La Messe pour le temps présent* projects our contemporary problems almost at random, suggesting vague solutions for some of them and putting question marks after others. I end the *Mass* by a pause, a period of waiting. I cannot myself say definitely what is its significance; it is up to the spectator to give the pause the sense that suits him personally.

It sometimes disturbs me when I myself have some doubts about a weakness in a work and a critic confirms that sense of weakness. But I don't give criticism much thought—I am not working for eternity. When a ballet no longer pleases me, I forget it and no one will be able to see it any more. Choreography must remain a kind of direct action comparable to a political action. Once it is no longer current, there is nothing left, other than the immediate memory of it among those who participated in it.

People sometimes accuse me of lacking respect in some of my works—for example, the picture I give of Baudelaire. To me, love is the only form of respect. One cannot betray when one loves. I love Baudelaire enough to knock him down and build him up again. I wanted to produce a work that would be an act of love towards a young man who was intensely modern. What is there to prove that historians and academics have more respect than I have for Baudelaire and his work?

I have been asked if I see common ground between Baudelaire and Nijinsky, since I have done biographies of both of them in dance. I find in both the same genius, the same anguish, and also the same wisdom in the midst of their follies. Both came to terrible ends because they

were prophets in advance of their times. Today, a creative genius has more chance of being revealed because values change so quickly. Before, a man could die without ever having been able to expound his thought. I personally have been fortunate. People laughed in my face when I was 20; I had my first successes at 30.

These days, I deliberately have no house, no little place in the country or by the sea. I have two rooms in Brussels without a telephone, with tons of records piled on the floor, and two suitcases in the hall. That's independence and freedom—to have two suitcases, hotels all over the world, and no possessions—ever.

I don't think freedom is indispensable to an act of creation, however, except, of course, a certain physical liberty—that people aren't put in prison, or made martyrs. But the creation of a work in fact *demands* a climate of violence and of searching: remember that the Italian Renaissance took place in the midst of war. One creates out of sorrow, not out of joy.

I don't enjoy going to ballet performances, because when I go to see a work I go to learn something. One

Above: Nijinsky, Clown of God, *with Jorge Donn as Nijinsky*

Over: Bhakti, *with Germinal Cassado and Maina Gielgud*

learns nothing from one's own *métier*—there is a sort of affective barrier. I learn more at the cinema or at a concert —I find it easier to take the point. A ballet performance doesn't extend me at all.

My current projects . . . I would like more and more to rediscover the atmosphere of celebration, and to help the public to take part and to express themselves. Dance has to become once again an integral part of our culture, as far as participation is concerned. To me, this doesn't exclude a more elaborate kind of dance, or the creation of ballets for performance in the theatre—but I do not want to pursue and complete my idea. It would demand that a generation of cripples rediscover the use of their legs. I have taken a lot of people to circuses and stadiums—now I want to make them dance, so that they have the taste for dancing about them. The aim of my life has always been to make a place for dance in civilization. I will have succeeded the day that the Minister of National Education makes dance compulsory in schools.

When I want to make the whole of Avignon dance I shall fill the different scenic spots destined to be part of the festival with companies which are specialists in research.

We shall install dance workshops where, under the direction of numerous teachers, it will be possible for all those who want, to come and work with the aim of ending the festival with a huge choreographic fête. I will be the means of bringing back public participation, of rediscovering the tradition that goes back to the festivals of Dionysus, which our own 17th century revived. Dancing is a magnificent means of union, of assimilation, of education. I prove this every day at the École Mudra which I founded in Brussels, where young people of 16 to 20 can open up both physically and morally. Dance being a source of regeneration for the human spirit, should not our role be to help the greatest number of people to benefit from it?

At the moment I am drawn towards the Greek theatre, because in establishing a perfect equilibrium between the rival magnetisms of words, music and dance, it knew how to capture all the audience's senses, and its intelligence too, and thereby enrich them. In Pericles' day a performance had none of the severity that we have come to attribute to it through the works of Seneca and our own classical authors. In fact, it was an odd, symbolic combination of pilgrimage and superbazaar, of the most joyful foolery and the most elevated fervour. I want to rediscover that spirit, to erase, as often as possible, the barrier that separates the actors from the audience, and invite all dancers of good will to join us on the other side of the footlights. Here, perhaps, is the last refuge in our world where a man can discover the exact measure of his own soul.

I think that people—especially young people—literally hurl themselves towards anything that is experimental and new. I proved this in New York recently. It was like a secret need for new emotions—that is always what I experience, on my part, from across the footlights—a quality of emotion, of love, of human contact . . . . I have never claimed to be avant-garde. What I have always seen in dance is an art that is simple, popular and direct. What I have always sought is a certain kind of truth in the relationship between stage and audience, and that this truth should touch people, ballet enthusiasts and uninitiated alike. It is really the uninitiated who interest me— those men and women who feel the need to rise at the end of my work to cry out to the dancers that they love them— as I have seen happen in New York. I cannot dream of anything better.

Left: Nijinsky, Clown of God
with Jorge Donn and Suzanne Farrell
Over: Le Sacre du Printemps
performed by the Ballet du
Vingtième Siècle
Right: Marcia Haydee of the
Stuttgart Ballet as Juliet in John
Cranko's Romeo and Juliet

Stuttgart Ballet

The Stuttgart Ballet, Germany's pride, is really the creation of John Cranko. South African born, a dancer and choreographer with the Royal Ballet for nearly fifteen years, Cranko had established himself as a man with an outstanding creative talent when, in 1961, he was appointed director of the ballet of the Stuttgart Opera House. He swiftly made the company internationally famous by producing an extraordinary range and quantity of ballets which stretched and developed the capabilities of his dancers to the full. The Stuttgart Ballet has triumphed all over Europe, in America and in the USSR. No small part of this success has been due to the presence of Marcia Haydee, a ballerina with an exquisite classical style and great dramatic power, and also to her partner Richard Cragun, who is an equally exciting dancer. In Egon Madsen the Stuttgart troupe boasts another quite exceptional male dancer, and in Birgit Keil a young ballerina of lovely and still developing talent. Cranko's sudden death in the summer of 1973 was a tragedy for the Stuttgart Ballet and for the ballet world.

Top left: Marcia Haydee as Juliet and Richard Cragun as Romeo in the balcony scene in Cranko's Romeo and Juliet.

Centre left: Marcia Haydee as Juliet in the ballroom scene

Left: Egon Madsen as the Joker in Cranko's Jeu de Cartes

Above: Marcia Haydee as Tatyana, with Heinz Clauss as Onegin, in Cranko's Eugene Onegin

Over above: Marcia Haydee and Egon Madsen in Giselle, Act I

Over below: The male corps de ballet in John Cranko's Mozart Concerto

Right: Marcia Haydee and Richard Cragun in the Taming of the Shrew *pas de deux which they danced at the Fanfare for Europe Gala at Covent Garden*

Below: Richard Cragun as Petrucchio

Ballet Théâtre Contemporain

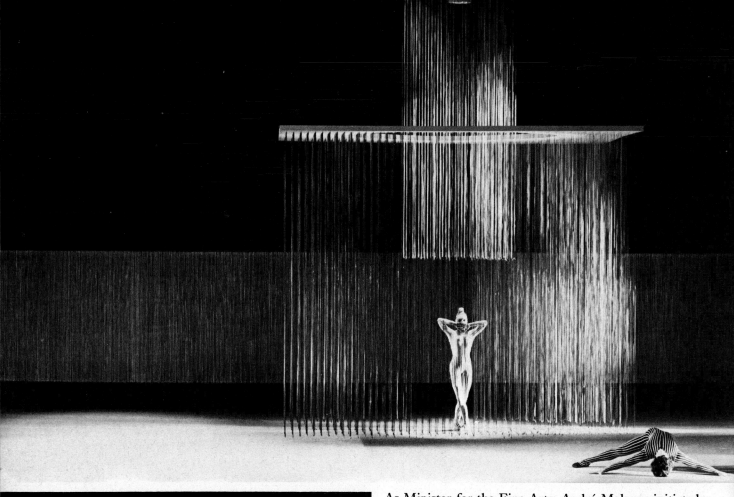

As Minister for the Fine Arts, André Malraux initiated a magnificent scheme of cultural centres situated throughout the French provinces. These *Maisons de la Culture* are complexes that can contain a theatre, recital room, library, and exhibition areas, and represent a most far-sighted attempt to involve each local community in the arts, as spectators and participants. Ballet Théâtre Contemporain was established at Amiens and is a troupe totally modern in outlook. The Director, Jean-Albert Cartier, ensures the collaboration of distinguished painters to decorate his company's ballets, and has sought the participation of some of the best of French and foreign choreographers and internationally celebrated composers. In 1972 the Ballet Théâtre Contemporain transferred to Angers as part of a national choreographic and operatic centre.

Previous page: Dancers of Ballet-Théâtre Contemporain in Hopop

Top: Martine Parmain and James Urbain in Michel Descombey's Violostries *designed by Jesus-Raphael Soto*

Centre: Pasdansés *by Dirk Sanders and René Goliard to music by Stravinsky and with scenery by Roman Cieslewicz*

Left: Requiem *by Françoise Adret, designed by Francisco Sobrino*

Rudi van Dantzig
The Dutch Inheritance

PEOPLE WHO HAVE SEEN MY WORKS
often criticize me for being a pessimist, someone who sees life and human behaviour darkly. "Throughout your choreographic career," they say, "you have given us various aspects of a sad philosophy, a gloomy opinion of what has been achieved and is happening in our world."

This may be true, and even this article may sound like a rather negative voice, yet I dare to say that I am not a pessimist and I certainly do not want audiences to react negatively to the experiences that come to them from the stage.

For centuries Holland has been a churchgoing, calvinistic nation; and people were accustomed to attend religious services, listen to sermons, and go home again, accepting everything that was told and read to them without discussion or doubt, but also without gladness. It was as if Christianity had been set on their shoulders like a rock, and silently, without grumbling, they carried it. If it did not seem to bring them joy or relief, neither did it cause any rebellion against a world which was far from being the way Christ had wished it to be.

Traditionally the Dutch are rather a silent nation; neither the British ease of conversation nor the brilliant discussion of which the French are masters, are ours. This may account for the fact that the frivolous dance is more popular with Dutch audiences than drama; dancers at least do not speak, and besides there is music! For music is the only art that is fully accepted in the Netherlands—the Concertgebouw Orchestra was already famous in times when dancers were considered mere fools. One of the great events in Holland's musical and social life is closely related to Dutch religious tradition; it is the annual Eastertime performance of Bach's *St Matthew Passion*. Over a period of two weeks some 50 concerts are given to packed halls. Young and old from all classes of the population gather for three and a half hours, listen in concentration to music and gospel, and leave without applauding, as if they were in church.

Having observed these audiences in the concert hall, I decided to use the final chorale of the *St Matthew Passion* to close my most recent ballet *Painted Birds*. I had been struck by the way we all seem to accept passively what is happening in and to the world today, just as people used to accept going to church, and as the people of Jerusalem had agreed to—or at least allowed—what happened there so long ago. While all the 50 dancers who have appeared in the ballet come together on stage in a motionless group and sing the final words of the chorale, a cinema screen at the back of the stage shows images of cruelty, egoism, thoughtlessness and destruction with which we are daily confronted in all kinds of media. Through the enormous discrepancy between the spirit of the music, the crudeness of the film, and the action of the dancers who stand

Previous page: A scene from Toer van Schayk's ballet Before, During and After the Party; *also top left, with Francis Sinceretti, Sonja Marchiolli and Pierre Althoff*

Centre: Nicolette Langestraat, Toer van Schayk, Erna Droog and Margriet van Waveren in Van Dantzig's Epitaph

solidly like a gigantic monument and finally abandon their art form—dance—for another—singing—I hoped to draw a strong reaction from the onlookers, an outspoken opinion, maybe a decision. It is always quite difficult to judge how strongly an audience is impressed: people simply applaud and leave the theatre.

In the case of *Painted Birds* there was sometimes no applause at all, but I received more reactions, in favour or opposed, than to any other ballet I made. Some people wanted to join the company on stage to give expression to their feelings of togetherness, others felt that the entire audience should get to their feet and sing with the dancers. There were also people who saw no point in seeing on the stage what they were already confronted with far too much, and who thought it was shocking and inhuman to show on film the suffering inflicted upon an animal by human beings.

In the case of another controversial Dutch work, the Netherlands Dance Theatre's production of *Mutations* by Glen Tetley and Hans van Manen, I am convinced that the naked, and at one time blood-smeared dancers were not meant by the choreographers merely to shock the audience. To me *Mutations* meant a view into a frightening future, with its images of space-possessed, space-tortured beings, dehumanized, in a world where the overgrowth of the

population causes violence, a cold, computerized civilization in crisis, where any human cry for help echoes back its own hollowness. The beauty and warmth of the human body, of human relationships, of quiet, simple love and trust seem out of reach, a fata morgana from the past. If a work, a choreography, has the effect of a seed planted in the earth, with the ability to grow, if a grain of that work is received by the spectator, who will develop it in his mind and form his own opinion and thoughts, then to me it means a double act of creation and the most worthwhile kind of creativity: to make people aware of their ideals and abilities, to strengthen their faith in what they can achieve.

Dance in the Netherlands is rather a contradictory subject, and to write or even to talk about it is not an easy thing. If a classical tradition existed in Amsterdam and The Hague during the 18th and 19th centuries, it was totally abandoned and forgotten during the hundred years that lasted, roughly, up to the Second World War. Dutch dance in the first half of the 20th century was marked by various styles of "free", German and Central European dance forms. Classical dance had its beginnings just after the Second World War, and in a country that is notably dance-minded its history was bound to be a difficult and often an unhappy one. Many people gave all their available energy and care, but they all suffered from

Far left: Han Ebbelaar in Rudi van Dantzig's Painted Birds

Above: Jessica Folkerts and René Vincent in the second act of Giselle *in the Dutch National Ballet's staging*

115

a lack of tradition and of knowledge; they did not have the basic foundations on which classical ballet is built.

However, thanks to their work, Holland, which is only a small country, has three ballet companies today: the Dutch National Ballet, the Netherlands Dance Theatre and the Scapino Ballet. The two youngest of them (the Dutch National Ballet is eleven, the Netherlands Dance Theatre ten years of age) have travelled a great deal all over the world and produced some internationally respected choreographers. They have also assembled a large repertory of classic as well as modern works enabling Dutch audiences to see many different aspects of choreographic art.

All three companies are state-supported and have good studios, and since one of their main duties consists of giving performances all over Holland, they are very lucky that splendid modern theatres have been, or are being built in many towns. The prices of Dutch theatre tickets are very moderate or cheap in comparison to those in most other countries, and there is a growing audience of ballet lovers.

All this sounds very hopeful and rewarding, and it certainly is, but—and here we touch on one of the contradictory aspects of the situation—the large tree seems to be short of roots. Somehow Holland has failed to form a school, an institution where young dancers can find the best possibilities of teaching and teachers, a concentration of the best that has been produced over the years. Although the government recognized the necessity to back the three main companies as much as possible, both morally and financially, they lacked the foresight or the initiative to understand that institutions like the Royal Ballet School in London, the Juilliard School in New York, or Leningrad's Kirov School are vital to the great companies of those cities.

The recognition the Dutch companies have received both in Holland and abroad, coupled with the number of successful works created by Dutch choreographers, may have suggested to most people that everything was going the right way. However, with the required standard and technical level of dancing getting steadily higher, all the companies are having more and more difficulty finding young Dutch dancers with sufficient schooling. Both the National Ballet and the Netherlands Dance Theatre seem to rely heavily on foreign talent, which is acceptable and rewarding where soloist dancers are concerned, but becomes alarming when even the lower ranks are a living symbol of the United Nations.

As Holland is not very frequently visited by foreign companies (it is years since we have seen the Royal Ballet, the New York City Ballet or the American Ballet Theater, and we have never had the Royal Danish Ballet or John Cranko's Stuttgart company), young Dutch dancers, and perhaps their teachers too, tend to lose contact with what is going on outside their country; this means they are often unaware of deficiencies in level or refinement of style in performance. This may also account for the fact that choreographers like Van Manen, Van Schayk or myself are often more strongly inspired by the other arts, such as film, literature, and painting or sculpture, than by the works of other choreographers.

Spectators who have seen various examples of Dutch contemporary choreography will not be surprised to learn that Hans van Manen is a collector of hard-edge art in the field of Stella and Vasarely, and generally keeps up with current art forms. He seems to have followed the tradition of Mondrian's squares: a spectator with a sharp eye may even have observed how the floor-patterns of Van Manen's choreographies design the forms of squares over the stage. My own inspiration lies in a totally different field, the distorted or subtly haunted worlds of Francis Bacon, David Hockney, Peter Blake and George Segal, perhaps with Van Gogh's last hallucinated works, his blue circling moons and decaying landscapes, as the origin of my work.

Toer van Schayk is just starting to explore his choreographic abilities, after experimenting with dancing and designing. He is an expert in Byzantine art and iconpainting and his works and thoughts seem to prepare themselves for the Last Judgement, whatever and whenever that may be. He draws a parallel between the very early arts and those of tomorrow through images of great sculptural beauty. His newest work *Before, During and After the Party* seems to me a piece with an overwhelming wealth of ideas and philosophies on what the dance should or could be. For many people his way of looking at things may seem unacceptable; for others, however, it will be a source of many inspirations and new ideas.

For both Toer van Schayk and myself films like Fellini's 8½, Pasolini's *Pigsty, Oedipus Rex,* and *St Matthew Passion,* and Bertolucci's *The Conformist* have definitely been inspiring, both in the way their works are constructed and deal with tensions, and in the intellectual and visual treatment and exposure of their subjects.

Jaap Flier, whom I practically grew up with in an artistic sense, and with whom I shared all the choreographic discoveries and excitements of our early dance years, is now the artistic director of the Netherlands Dance Theatre. We both started as beginning choreographers in the same programme in January 1955, he with a work inspired by Kafka's *The Trial,* I with the Martha Graham-inspired *Night Island.* Flier and I are both meeting with the same difficulties and anxieties: trying to be creative and to produce new works, while at the same time having to guide our respective companies through the hazards of endless rehearsals, tours abroad and some 150 performances a year each in Holland.

It seems curious to me, yet at the same time logical, to realize that Flier and I, after so many years, are back in the same position, facing the same difficulties and dealing with the same problems as we used to encounter in miniature, when our first teacher and directress, Sonia Gaskell, would push the young boys we then were to try and show Dutch audiences our first steps in the labyrinths of choreography.

Sonia Gaskell did more for classical dance in Holland than anybody else. It was she who started, more or less on her own, propagating her ideals in a country which up till then had been imbued with the influence of German "free dance" and the belief that personality and self-

expression were far superior to the discipline and stern rigidity of the classical training. Sonia Gaskell audiences in Holland were aware not only of the beauty and artistic riches of Petipa and Fokine, but also the existence of Massine, Balanchine, Jooss and Béjart, to mention but a few. She gave the dance in Holland its wings and helped it in its first efforts to fly.

The creative tradition of dance in Holland has always been and still is far from entertaining: neither the choice of music nor the choice of subjects seems easy. Like the hippies in Holland, who could not be satisfied with flower power alone, and so started a political party and got involved in the real problems of Dutch society like traffic, housing and city planning, the choreographers explore and go their lonely ways.

Is it the inheritance of a joyless Calvinistic church, and is that church itself a reaction to that small flat piece of land where water always seems ready to come in from above, from underneath and from the sides? Dark water is what we have, and endless horizons in an enormous sky of ever-changing clouds, and flat meadows with a choreography of flying birds above. That seems to me the soil from which our dance stems.

Dance, because it is without language, is an international language which every human being is able to understand— and it should be used as such. Through the ages there have been messages in dance—symbols, signs and emotions which have had the power to strike people, and which they recognized as the truth. The dance has many sides and many faces; it is the heartbeat of the human being in time. Each country, each era, has a unique contribution to make. I hope that of the dance-world of the Netherlands is a worthy facet of this marvellous whole.

Above: Rudi van Dantzig's Moments, *with Martina Frei, Istvan Matula, Sonja Marcakci*

Above: Alexandra Radius and Han Ebbelaar in Hans van Manen's Twilight, *created for the Dutch National Ballet*

Nederlands Dans Theater

The Nederlands Dans Theater is one of the most productive ballet companies in the world: for many years its yearly staging of new ballets averaged ten. Completely modern in outlook, adventurous, and with a consistent and distinctive dance style, the troupe has earned world acclaim for the distinction of its dancers and for the quality of its stagings. Many of the productions were created by Hans van Manen, who was for several years the artistic director of the company.

Left: Anja Licher and Gérard Lemaître in Mutations *by Glen Tetley and Hans van Manen*
*Top: * Situation *by Hans van Manen*

Above: Susan Kenniff and Hans Knill and the soprano Anne Haenen who sings a solo by John Cage in Hans van Manen's ballet Solo for Voice I

Top: Kathy Gosschalk and Tony Hulbert in Hans van Manen's Three Pieces
Centre: Glen Tetley's Imaginary Film *with Harmen Tromp and*

Leon Koning

Above: Jaap Flier with Willy de la Bije in Glen Tetley's Anatomy Lesson

Royal Danish Ballet

It is only during the past twenty years that the world outside Denmark has really become aware of the magnificence of the ballet in Copenhagen. The founder of the greatness of the Danish ballet is August Bournonville (1805–1879) whose ballets have been lovingly preserved and remain a touching and powerful testimony to his genius. His system of training dancers—the French noble style which he inherited from Auguste Vestris, his teacher—is the continuing basis for the Danes' eminence. The Danes have always welcomed foreign choreographers and the Copenhagen repertory today combines works by Bournonville and by Flemming Flindt—now director of the company—with many of the most influential creators of this century.

Top left: Kirsten Simone and Henning Kronstam in Swan Lake

Left: Niels Kehlet and Solveig Ostergaard in a typical Bournonville jump from Napoli

Above: Flemming Flindt re-staged Swan Lake *for his company: Anna Laerkesen as Odette*

Centre: The Lifeguards on Amager is Bournonville's memorial to the volunteer force that defended the Danish coast from Lord Nelson and the British Navy. Here the Lifeguards, led by Kjeld Noack, are met by a local farmer mimed by Poul Vessel
Right: Ole Fatum, Flemming Flindt as the Wolf-man, and Vivi Flindt as the girl in Roland Petit's Le Loup

121

Nadia Nerina Visit to Russia

*I*N THE BOLSHOI THEATRE DRESSING room, the long white dressing table is covered with a chaos of makeup sticks, powder, hair nets, pins, jars of removing cream, cotton wool and tissues, and supports a vast mirror surrounded by bright, naked bulbs which have heated the air, permeating it with the smell of melted greasepaint and powder.

I stare at my face in the mirror, which up till now has been the pale, tragic visage of Odette, Queen of the Swans. Now smeared with grease and a profusion of mingled colours, it is a strange sight as I slowly wipe off the makeup. This is a moment somehow suspended in time. The removal of each section of makeup seems to expunge days of rehearsal, excitement, tensions, anxiety, apprehension for the evening that has just been. I am hot, excited, tired and very happy as the pins are slowly taken out of my hair, and the dressing gown clings damp and comforting to my body.

Galina Ulanova, the greatest living ballerina, has just slipped quietly out of my dressing room. She had come, after everyone else had left, to tell me how much pleasure my performance has given her, and to congratulate me on my interpretation of the role of Odette-Odile in one of the classical repertoire's greatest ballets, *Swan Lake*. Hers are words of approval and praise I shall cherish all my life.

It was a morning in June 1960 and the sun was streaming through the windows of our house in Kensington when the letter arrived from Russia inviting me to dance *Giselle* at the Kirov Theatre in Leningrad, partnered by the company's director, Konstantin Sergeyev, and *Swan Lake* at the Bolshoi Theatre in Moscow, with the *premier danseur* Nikolai Fadeyechev. Speechless, I handed the letter to my husband. We were both equally overwhelmed by this completely unexpected invitation.

Dame Ninette de Valois, director of our company, immediately made arrangements so that I would be free to appear in Russia in October. I would dance as scheduled with the Royal Ballet in New York in September in *La Fille mal Gardée*, *Swan Lake* and *The Sleeping Beauty*, later rejoining the company in Chicago for the remainder of its five months' tour of America.

When we arrived at Moscow Airport I was surprised and pleased to be welcomed by Mr Orvid, a portly, jovial man who was the Bolshoi Theatre's director. He came forward and greeted me warmly, and the slim attractive girl at his side interpreted that he was welcoming me on my first visit to Moscow and wishing me every success for a splendid season with his company. I was presented with armfuls of flowers and photographed from every angle. When the luggage had been collected we were ushered into a large car and set off for Moscow, followed by a fleet of cars carrying all the other theatre officials and dancers.

Moscow, like most other big cities, is sprawling, and we went through many winding streets. At last we arrived in Red Square, and the first familiar sight which greeted us was the famous St Basil's Church, with its many multi-coloured onion-shaped domes; next to it were the high walls that surround the Kremlin and, on the left, GUM, the famous and enormous department store.

I could hardly wait to see the Bolshoi Theatre, but Mrs Blackwell, who had accompanied me as my dresser, wisely insisted that we should first unpack and have a rest. At last, wrapped up warmly in our heavy coats, boots, fur hats and gloves, we set off from the hotel to trudge out into the deep snow which was still falling softly. Lights sparkled all round the square and the evening was quite magical.

After about five minutes' brisk walk, we turned a corner and stood still, drawing in our breaths. There in front of us was the Bolshoi Theatre with its monumental columns, surmounted by a gorgeous golden chariot drawn by four golden galloping horses. The theatre was floodlit and looked absolutely magnificent standing out against the white of the snow.

As we reached the steps the audience started coming out, and we realized that the evening performance was over. We slipped past the crowds, up the steps and into the foyer. Then we climbed the beautiful marble staircase, until we reached the promenade foyer with its vaulted, elaborately decorated ceiling and many chandeliers. During each interval it is the custom for the audience to stroll slowly around this foyer in twos and threes, discussing the merits of the previous act. At this point we felt sure that we would be stopped. However,

Previous page: Nadia Nerina in conversation with Yuri Faier the conductor, during her Moscow season, watched by Nikolai Fadeyechev

Left: Nadia Nerina and Nikolai Fadeyechev in Giselle, *Act II*

no one seemed to take any notice, so we quickly slipped into the auditorium itself.

It was a tremendous thrill to see this circular auditorium, decorated in gold and white and adorned with a myriad cut-glass chandeliers. The proscenium is vast and an enormous red-patterned curtain cascades down from beneath a mass of flags fanning out from a central motif— a portrait of Lenin encircled by a wreath. The stage is about half the size again of that of the Royal Opera House in London, which is large by any standards. So the Bolshoi Theatre certainly lives up to its name, which means 'big' in Russian.

With great excitement we sat down and gazed about us. I could not believe that in just a few nights I would be dancing there. Only when the last of the audience were filing out did we get up to follow.

That night I tossed and turned, thinking about the new choreography I would have to learn in such a short time. I was satisfied finally with my decision to teach the Bolshoi our interpretation and choreography of the Black Swan *pas de deux* in the third act, which I believe to have far greater dramatic impact than the Bolshoi version. I, in turn, would dance the fourth act exactly as it was presented in Moscow. The second act would be simple, as both companies danced practically identical versions, except for one or two inserted Bolshoi lifts which I felt were unnecessary and did not add to the poetry of the lakeside scene. These I would change, and would revert to our own gentler and simpler lifts onto the Prince's shoulder. This arrangement, I thought, would certainly be a diplomatic exchange of ideas between the two companies' productions, and would in no way alter the dramatic theme of the ballet as a whole. With these thoughts whirling around in my head I gradually fell asleep.

Next morning we were up early, and armed with my practice clothes and ballet shoes, we went to the theatre. I could not wait to have a glimpse of the stage, so Mr Orvid took me directly into the box. I noticed that in its centre was a table, surrounded by chairs, which was spread with a white cloth and topped by a huge silver swan.

As I peered over the edge of the box there were only the working lights on in the vast, gaping stage and in the auditorium all the chairs were covered with white dust sheets, looking for all the world as if the snow had floated down upon them during the night. After we had discussed the times of classes and rehearsals I was taken to the dressing room, descending the winding stairs and a confusion of backstage passages until we emerged onto the stage itself. It seemed even larger with all the decor cleared away in preparation for the morning's rehearsals. There was an army of blue-aproned ladies washing it with mops and pails. The air was fresh and clean, and I learned that special machinery was used to keep it so. From the stage we made our way through a large red-carpeted cor-ridor, where we were met by dancers rushing about in all directions. They wore long, flowing pink tunics down to their knees, quite different from the leotards we in the West are accustomed to wearing.

I shared a section of the dressing room with Raissa Struchkova, whom I had admired greatly when she appeared with the Bolshoi in London in 1956. She welcomed me warmly, kissing me on both cheeks. There were many other dancers there too, chatting and laughing while they changed; I recognized faces, although I did not as yet know all their names. They were fascinated by my ballet shoes. In the West all our shoes are made by Italian shoemakers, whose fathers have handed down their craft over the centuries. Ballet as we know it evolved in Italy, where the first "toe shoes" were introduced to enable such illustrious dancers as Taglioni, Grisi, Grahn and Cerrito to stay for a few seconds poised on their toes, giving the divine illusion of lightness. The Italian-made shoes even today are much lighter in construction than the shoes currently made in Russia.

Raissa mentioned that although we all shared the dressing rooms for classes and studio rehearsals, for the performance the ballerina appearing that night dressed in a large private dressing room farther down the corridor. The bells were ringing now, calling us for class, and hurriedly we took the lift to the top of the theatre. Class was held in the larger of the two rehearsal rooms, which was the same size as the stage, with an identical rake. It had vast windows and was light and airy, with a bar around three sides of the room and mirrors right across the fourth wall.

Right: Natalia Bessmertnova and Mikhail Lavrovsky in Yuri Grigorovich's version of The Nutcracker *for the Bolshoi Ballet.*

It was crowded and there was a marked air of tension and excitement. I was placed at the bar between Maya Plisetskaya and Raissa Struchkova. Taking the class was Marina Semyonova, who had been the Bolshoi's prima ballerina before Ulanova.

My technique was regarded with the utmost interest. We dancers in England are swifter, lighter and more precise than the Bolshoi dancers, whose movements are more fluid and elegiac. What seemed to surprise them most was that my training embraced the characteristics of their style while retaining the attributes of the British school. The strength of the Bolshoi style emanates from the supple, strong, but pliant use of the back, giving the dancers a complete freedom of movement which is nevertheless wholly disciplined and controlled.

It is a policy of the Bolshoi company to encourage and allow the ballerinas slight variations of the set choreography which will enhance both their personal attributes as dancers and their individual interpretations. So, during the rehearsals, I was fascinated when, on occasions, Marina Semyonova (who was coaching us) offered me a choice of choreographic variations: the version which she herself had danced as the greatest exponent of the role in her time and the version currently being danced by Maya Plisetskaya. Although I had seen the film of the Russian *Swan Lake* in London and had greatly admired Maya's exotic rendering of Odette and the fiery Odile, with her superb extensions and technique, she was in style a completely different artist from myself and I realized that our performances, even within the same framework, would be quite unlike each other. Therefore I invariably chose to learn Semyonova's version, for my approach to the role of Odette-Odile was entirely in sympathy with her reading of it.

What impressed me most when working with the Bolshoi dancers was the all-pervading atmosphere of serenity and tranquillity. I was also struck by the emphasis that Soviet ballet places on music. The producers feel, quite rightly, that unless the music is played superlatively well by an understanding conductor the performance invariably suffers, no matter how lavish the production or how brilliant the dancing. For me, too, the conductor is always of the greatest importance, and in Yuri Faier, I personally felt the company had one of the very few great conductors in the history of the ballet.

Top left: Maya Plisetskaya as Odette and Nikolai Fadeyechev as Siegfried in the second act of Swan Lake. *Left: Plisetskaya and Fadeyechev in* Swan Lake, *Act III. Plisetskaya, the supreme Bolshoi ballerina, dominates this ballet with an imperious grandeur and powerful lyric force that is unique in the world today*

Top right: Mikhail Lavrovsky as Albrecht horror-struck by the death of Giselle (Natalia Bessmertnova) in the Bolshoi Ballet's production.

Right: Maris Liepa as the villainous Crassus in Grigorovich's massive and spectacular piece, Spartacus, *with the Bolshoi Ballet*

Far right: Mikhail Lavrovsky, son of the famous choreographer Leonid Lavrovsky, is an outstanding artist even among the magnificent younger generation of Soviet dancers, and his interpretation of the heroic slave hero of Spartacus *is hailed as one of the greatest male performances of our time*

Left: Maya Plisetskaya as Kitri in Act I of Don Quixote *at a BBC television presentation of the Bolshoi Ballet. Plisetskaya's fantastic jumps and the exuberant brilliance of her technique bring this old ballet vividly to life*

Below left: Ekaterina Maximova, an outstanding Giselle of the Bolshoi Ballet who had been coached in the role by that great interpreter Galina Ulanova, with Maris Liepa as Albrecht: a scene from a television presentation of the second act

Top right: The celebrated corps de ballet of the Kirov Ballet in the Kingdom of Shades scene from Petipa's La Bayadère

Below right: Irina Kolpakova and Vladilen Semenyov in the Vision Scene from The Sleeping Beauty. *The Kirov Ballet maintains the Petipa classics with all the love and honour due to these great works which were created for the company when it was the Russian Imperial Ballet.* The Sleeping Beauty *was the most celebrated ballet of the 19th century and the Kirov production of the masterpiece is a leading repertory piece*

Far right: Alla Ossipienko and Jonny Markovsky in Swan Lake, *Act III, at the Kirov Theatre*

Following pages:
Top left: Maya Plisetskaya as the Dying Swan
Top right: A view from the wings of Nina Sorokina in the Bolshoi Ballet's display of transcendental technique: School of Ballet
Below left: A favourite show-piece in the Bolshoi Ballet's divertissement programme is the Polonaise and Krakoviak from Glinka's opera A Life for the Tsar (Ivan Susanin). *Here artists of the Bolshoi ballet are seen in the Polonaise*
Below right: Larissa Trembovelskaya in her Gipsy Dance, a solo from one of the Bolshoi divertissement programmes
Far right: Ludmilla Vlassova and Stanislav Vlassov in The Doves, *another work from the Bolshoi divertissement programmes*

Faier was also a most gentle and kind man, loved and revered by all. Although he was beginning to feel his age, and suffered from bad vision, he nevertheless insisted on attending every rehearsal and on many occasions accompanying the dancers at the piano with amazing energy. The help he gave me was invaluable. In the afternoon I had to teach Nikolai Fadeyechev our version of the third act. I was prepared for this, but not for the discovery that at the same time I had to teach it step by step to Yuri Faier. I held his hand and went through the entire *pas de deux* step by step, singing the tempi and then the solo and coda. I was amazed to find that he memorized it choreographically as quickly as Nikolai, and by the end of the afternoon we were all rehearsing as though they had never known another version of either choreography or tempi.

When I was invited to dance with the Bolshoi one of my reasons for accepting so confidently was that I would be partnered by Nikolai Fadeyechev, with whom I had already worked in London in 1958 when he was invited to partner me in the BBC's production of *Giselle*. Not only was he a superb partner, but when we danced it was one of those rare instances where two people move instinctively with the same rhythm. I believe that it is this natural coordination between a particular ballerina and *premier danseur*, uniting their every movement in harmony, which creates a special magic. I have been partnered by many great *premiers danseurs* but I have only experienced this natural rhythmical rapport with Alexis Rassine and Nikolai Fadeyechev.

All the next day we concentrated on the fourth act. This was both fascinating and exhausting because I had to learn not only the new choreography, but also to become accustomed to music I had not heard before, and those passages which were familiar became even more confusing with entirely different sequences of steps set to them.

Also my Western fundamental poetic belief that it is the Prince's sacrifice of his life for true love which reunites the lovers after death had to be reconciled with the Soviet approach of good prevailing over evil by the Prince's killing of Von Rothbart, and so uniting the lovers on earth. This entirely changed concept of the ballet's ending necessitated my rethinking, and altering my interpretation.

On the fifth day, after a run right through the ballet on the stage, Mrs Blackwell and I carefully arranged all my makeup in the large dressing room at the end of the corridor, ready for the performance the following day. The shoes I would wear for each act were carefully tried and retried and then laid out in order: the quieter, softer pair for Act II, with an extra pair should I prefer them, a couple of harder pairs for the strenuous third act, and two pairs for Act IV. The fastenings were carefully checked on the *tutus;* then, with a final glance around, we

Top left: Kaleriya Fedicheva as the Young Girl in Igor Belsky's Leningrad Symphony. *This work is a heart-rending visualization of Shostakovich's seventh symphony, celebrating the heroism of the* people of Leningrad under attack and siege by the Germans during the war
Left: Vadim Gulyayev in the third act of Oleg Vinogradov's Goryanka *at the Kirov Theatre*

hurried off to meet Nikolai and the other dancers in the theatre canteen.

I had been particularly impressed by the entire company's enthusiasm and interest in helping and encouraging me, even when the rehearsals had run well over the allotted time. There was never any pressure to finish until everyone was satisfied that we had achieved all we could. Everything possible was done to see that I would have confidence in my new surroundings to give of my very best in the performance.

On Sunday, I awoke to a beautiful day with the snow glistening in the sunshine. As always before a performance, I was tense with nervous excitement, my hands and feet ice-cold and restless, my mind entirely preoccupied with the role for that evening. We had a brisk walk in the tingling fresh air, and an enforced light lunch of meat and salad—so difficult to swallow. My clothes were carefully laid out for the evening, the heavy curtains drawn, then under the warm coverlet I gazed up at the ceiling, a disciplined calming process until I gradually relaxed into a deep, short sleep. Refreshed and composed, I got up and dressed quickly. Mrs Blackwell had tea ready, and we went off to the theatre. On the threshold of the stage door, I took a long, deep breath of the cold night air, then entered . . . .

Yuri Faier conducted that night and his orchestra's rendering of Tchaikovsky's beautiful music helped more than anything to make me feel wonderfully within the role. Nikolai Fadeyechev's partnering was, as always, all that one could wish. The ovation at the end of the performance was one of the longest, warmest and most endearing I have ever received.

After we had been called back to the stage repeatedly, surrounded by the assembled company, many of whom seemed to be in tears of delight, Leonid Lavrovsky, the Bolshoi's artistic director, took both my hands in his. Speaking with the deepest emotion, he told me, "Tonight was an outstanding one in the history of the Bolshoi and one we shall always remember and cherish. We are particularly happy that Moscow has so taken you to its heart, for we shall never forget our own rapturous welcome in London in 1956, and tonight we are extremely happy to be able to return this welcome to you in the same measure."

I thanked him and the company for the warm, openhearted affection bestowed upon me. Although both our companies could learn equally from each other, we as the younger company looked towards them as a daughter might look to her mother.

The audience was still applauding rapturously and patiently, so Fadayechev and I took a final call, stepping through the massive curtains on to the stage, which was strewn with flowers showered from all sides.

Top right: Irina Kolpakova as Eve and Mikhail Barishnikov as Adam in the three-act Creation of the World *by Natalia Kasatkina and Vladimor Vasilyov*
Right: Mikhail Barishnikov in Vestris, *a set of dance studies written for him by Leonid Jacobson. Barishnikov, most dazzling of the young generation of Kirov men, is a classic dancer of seemingly faultless style and prodigious virtuosity*

133

Right: Yuri Solovyov soaring in
Le Corsaire: *a rehearsal shot
at an Italian open-air theatre with
a set ready for* Aida

Above: Irina Kolpakova as
Aurora *in the* Sleeping Beauty
Act I

John Lanchbery
The Conductor's Work

BALLET SCORES FALL INTO THREE MAIN categories. Some scores have been specially composed for a specific scenario (Tchaikovsky's *The Sleeping Beauty* or Benjamin Britten's *The Prince of the Pagodas*); others were originally written as concert music and have been wedded later to ballets, either with a story (Frank Martin's Harpsichord Concerto, for example, was used by Kenneth MacMillan in setting Garcia Lorca's *Las Hermanas*) or in the abstract genre of pure dancing (as in César Franck's Symphonic Variations choreographed by Frederick Ashton). The third category of scores are selections from a composer's works made up to suit the particular needs of the choreographer (usually for a story ballet, as in John Cranko's *Pineapple Poll*, which was set to Sullivan extracts arranged by Charles Mackerras). This last type of ballet score, the *mélange*, had its origins in Fokine's use of a variety of Chopin's music for his ballet *Chopiniana*, which was first mounted in 1908. Since then many composers of the 18th, 19th, and even 20th century—from Bach (*The Wise Virgins*) to Mompou (*House of Birds*)—have proved fruitful sources for the choreographer and his musical arranger. But with the rapidly increasing complexity of modern music choreographers will be less likely to want this kind of score, for today's music does not readily lend itself to "twenty-four bars of this, a modulation in suitable style, and sixteen bars of that". Nor indeed are today's composers likely to permit such musical patchwork.

It is important to consider how dancers rehearse a ballet, in terms of music and choreography. Ballet is the one performing art that is taught by word of mouth. It is true that a number of systems of choreographic notation have been in use for many years, but at any rehearsal to this day a notation is used (if at all) by one person—an interpreter as it were—who has the gift, which most dancers do not possess, of reading it. Painstakingly, he explains the movements and patterns to the individual dancers literally step by step in exactly the same way as an early jazz composer and band leader like Jelly-Roll Morton would go round his group singing each individual melody or harmony in his composition to the musician concerned, who would then learn his part by ear. Sometimes there are differences of opinion between the choreologist and dancers who have taken part in that ballet before. The notations do not seem to be quite perfect as yet, and dancers have stubborn memories. So one can readily assess how many hours have to go into reviving even a short ballet after it has been dropped from the repertory for a while. With a new ballet the process is even slower, for a choreographer suffering the pangs of creation can rarely invent even a minute of good new choreography in an hour.

All this means that dancers have to have a simplified version of the music to work to, and until about 90 years ago this used to be provided by two violinists. I have seen part of the violin duet rehearsal copy of *Swan Lake*, and it makes fascinating musical reading! The first ballet in France to be rehearsed to a piano was Messager's *The Two Pigeons* (1886); but since that time the piano has taken the place of the violin duet, and today the rehearsal pianist is a supremely important figure in any ballet company.

The first-rate rehearsal pianist is worth his weight in gold. By keeping one eye on the dancers, he will learn, if not the substance, at least the appearance of the choreography so that he knows where in the music the dancers wish to resume after the frequent breaks in the rehearsal; he will work in collaboration with the *répétiteur* or choreographer, who naturally tends to think choreographically rather than musically, or when he does think musically will often favour pulse rhythm and tempo at the expense of line phrasing and form. The pianist has to play the same few bars of music, often an incomplete phrase, over and over again with the same inflections—or deliberately different ones to suit the requirements of a different dancer sharing a role; he must try at the same time to keep faith with the composer and his original intentions; and he must avoid treating the music pianistically (except, of course, where the music demands it). I have often noticed that pianists tend to have trouble with orchestral music which translates badly for piano. For instance, the end of Aurora's Variation in the last act of *The Sleeping Beauty*, with its quick leaps from low octave *A*'s to high tonic chords is not easy on the piano. An average pianist is tempted to slow down slightly so as not to play wrong notes, whereas a good *rehearsal* pianist will take a chance and maintain the tempo. Failure to do this will lead the

Top: Sir Frederick Ashton's La Fille mal Gardée *has now entered the repertory of the Australian Ballet: Marilyn Jones as Lise, in the second scene of Act I*

Centre: Marilyn Rowe and corps de ballet in Rudolf Nureyev's staging of Don Quixote *for the Australian Ballet*

Right: Antony Tudor has worked with the company, and created The Divine Horseman *for the troupe*

Following pages; left: Marilyn Jones and Garth Welch in Petipa's Raymonda, *a staging by Rudolf Nureyev for the Australian Ballet*

dancer to expect a *rallentando* there, and time will be wasted later at the rehearsal with orchestra while she asks for one from the conductor—who could probably have spent more time at the studio rehearsals anyway!

The good rehearsal pianist marks the rehearsal score liberally with all sorts of signposts: pet names for certain step sequences (the "flying seven", the "I-want-to-be-happy" bit), action and pattern guides ("four girls to up-stage left"), and, in the case of ballets with mime, even the indicated dialogue ("over there a lake—my mother's tears"). The most important marks of all are the "counts" —the number of easily countable beats into which each phrase or part-phrase can be broken up. To count or not to count has sometimes been a vexed question in the past: one director I know started a new season, after years of rehearsing by counts, with the startling announcement that the dancers could no longer be allowed to count but must learn the musical phrasing by heart. A few weeks later she was busily rehearsing the revival of a ballet very dear to her with all the old counts, including a series of un-musical ones which had been hallowed by time! Dancers learn these counts in long sequences, rather like a string of telephone numbers. Thus a section of Stravinsky's *The Rite of Spring*, for example, will be remembered as "two nines, a seven, a four, three fives, a slow four and an eleven". I've heard this commented on with horror by a purist musician, but it certainly makes an unbeatable *aide-mémoire* for those poor dancers who have to perform this difficult work from memory. Would the musician care to play *Rite* without his music?

The piano is able to convey the sounds and effects of much modern orchestral music: certainly the Stravinsky ballets rehearse well to a piano, and its uniquely percussive

Right : Vanessa Harwood and Sergiu Stefanschi in Erik Bruhn's production of Swan Lake *for the National Ballet of Canada*

Below : Rudolf Nureyev's staging of The Sleeping Beauty *for the National Ballet of Canada with designs by Nicholas Georgiadis*

Australian Ballet

The Australian Ballet's inaugural season took place in Sydney in November 1962, and since then the company has won acclaim throughout the world as well as in its homeland where it performs in every major city of Australia and New Zealand. The directors, Dame Peggy van Praagh and Sir Robert Helpmann had both played vital parts in the development of the Royal Ballet, and the Australian Ballet is inevitably influenced—as is the Canadian National Ballet—by the English national company and school created by Dame Ninette de Valois. However the Australian company is in no sense a copy or an imitation of the British ensemble: it is essentially Australian, and admired as such throughout the world.

quality sometimes gives a better rhythmic drive than the orchestral sound it is representing. But a lot of modern orchestral music goes beyond the possibilities of a piano reduction, and the increasing popularity of the tape recorder has led to its use in ballet rehearsals. As a conductor I cannot help regretting this for reasons I will explain in a moment.

So far I have said little about the ballet conductor's role in rehearsals. He can certainly help a great deal in a new ballet's creation, for choreographers tend to do strange things with music. (A musician might be amazed at what Balanchine did to the well-known *Serenade for Strings* of Tchaikovsky—making a long, unbalancing repeat in the Waltz, boiling down a passage of modulating progression in the Finale by cutting every other two bars of it, and even transposing the order of the last two movements. But the resulting ballet is superb!) The conductor can learn considerably from attendance at the ballet rehearsal studio, for he too must know his way around the choreography and the musical problems it presents to the dancers.

If the company has been well rehearsed to a piano their first run with orchestra should give them a "lift", an exciting feeling of suddenly being near to actual performance. This lift, alas, is absent if they have rehearsed to tape, for a live orchestra in a theatre pit cannot help but sound thin by comparison. Even more important is the stifling effect on a conductor's musicianship of not being able to mould a performance after his own heart but having instead to try to duplicate a taped performance, which is usually that of another conductor.

Of course recorded tape is now being used by composers of electronic music as the end product in itself, thereby doing away altogether with the conductor and orchestra in performance. As yet combination of taped electronic sounds, music and live orchestra has not been fully exploited—a fascinating work in this genre, a sort of tape-recorder concerto, is Roberto Gerhard's *Collages*, which was used by MacMillan for his ballet *Checkpoint*. At present we cannot pretend that electronic music as we know it appeals to more than a small fraction of the public: in fact I have this very year heard a ballet audience be noisily disapproving. Electronic music also poses problems to both choreographers and dancers. Composers occasionally forget that one of their first duties is to communicate, and choreographers are sometimes tempted to use music that frankly they do not understand and consequently cannot come to grips with, simply because it is avant-garde. As an easy way out, the choreography is sometimes reduced to a sort of slow writhing with an occasional sharp movement from a dancer frantically listening for his "plink" or "grrrm" to match it to, while the more subtle rhythmic and formal elements are glossed over or ignored. At one recent performance of an ultra-modern ballet by a well-known company the poor dancers, trying to fit

Top left: Gailene Stock as the girl in Helpmann's The Display, *a ballet which finds analogies between the behaviour of young people and the mating ritual of the lyre-bird*

Left: Sir Robert Helpmann's ballet Sun Music, *with a specially commissioned score by Peter Sculthorpe, and designs by Kenneth Rowell*

nebulous choreography to an equally nebulous electronic score—and perhaps wanting to get on with the rest of the programme—gradually got more and more ahead of the music. The stage manager watching from the prompt corner saw with alarm that the dancers were taking the final position when there was still a minute and a half of the tape to run. With great presence of mind he faded out the unfinished cacophony and discreetly brought down the curtain. Surely the art of ballet should add up to more than this!

Live modern music entails fresh difficulties, for not only is the music itself growing more complex, but composers are tending to write for ever stranger and wilder combinations. Theatre orchestra pits are of limited size, yet now music is being written for three or four different orchestras all playing at once! Nor is the increasing use of the improvisatory element in music likely to make for a closer unity between the composer and the choreographer, and that, after all, is what is lacking in so much modern ballet. These days it is so easy to go to any good record shop and buy a performance of practically anything, and this is where the trouble begins, for as I have said music is sometimes tempting to a choreographer simply because of its modernity. He may well get vibrations and wonderful images from his first hearing of it (in fact, he would not be much of a choreographer if he did not), but the final result is all too often not what modern ballet should be.

The answer surely lies in tempting today's composers to write ballet scores. Commissions are all-important, and money and courage must be found for them. Choreographers must have worthwhile ideas, and learn to develop their flair and spirit to suit today's music and discover how to complement it with their art. For his part the composer must be willing to adapt, rewrite and recolour his new score in collaboration with the choreographer, and to write for the musical forces that are readily available. I am sure that a lot of wonderful music can still be written for a comparatively normal-sized orchestra and a sufficiently competent conductor without doing violence to a composer's unique way of expressing himself. Lastly, we should not forget the dancers. Somehow they must be educated to a different musical level. Perhaps they could do one or two of their ballet classes each week to music that is much more advanced than the usual polkas, waltzes and tangos; or they could have two classes a day, one primarily balletic, and the other to an accompaniment highlighting new musical thought. Perhaps the company of the future should have a whole section of its dancers— those suitably talented to do so—who concentrate on modern works, instead of constantly switching, as at present, from classical to modern and back to classical. This probably means materially increasing the number of dancers. But then I am always being told that there are too few jobs for too many dancers anyway.

Right: Veronica Tennant as the Sylphide and Niels Kehlet, a guest from the Royal Danish Ballet, as James in Bournonville's La Sylphide *produced by National Ballet of Canada*

National Ballet of Canada

Celia Franca, a distinguished dancer with the Royal Ballet and with Ballet Rambert, went to Canada at the suggestion of Dame Ninette de Valois to help found the National Ballet of Canada in Toronto in 1949. The company, which she still directs, has absorbed the original inspiration from the Royal Ballet, and has developed in an individual fashion to become Canada's finest dance company, an impression confirmed by the National Ballet's first triumphant overseas tour in 1972. One other significant fact is that the School of the National Ballet of Canada is recognized throughout the world as one of the finest ballet academies.